WORKBOOK

GLENCOE
LATIN 1

LATIN
FOR AMERICANS

Glencoe

New York, New York   Columbus, Ohio   Chicago, Illinois

The McGraw-Hill Companies

Send all inquiries to:
Glencoe/McGraw-Hill
8787 Orion Place
Columbus, OH 43240-4027

ISBN: 0-07-829222-0

Printed in the United States of America.

13 14 15 16 17 RHR 15 14 13

CONTENTS

UNIT V

UNIT VI

UNIT VII

UNIT VIII

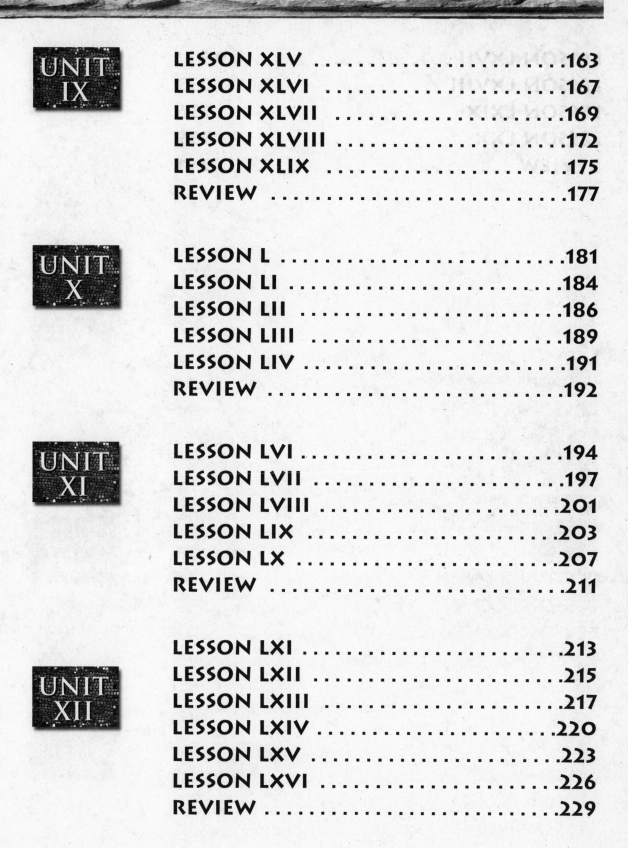

UNIT XIII

UNIT I

THE ROMAN WORLD: ROMAN ITALY

LESSON I

RŌMA ET ITALIA

A **Pronunciation: long and short vowels** Your textbook introduces you to the way that Latin was probably spoken by the ancient Romans (pages 9–11). You may extend your pronunciation practice with the following words. Most are in the dictionary of your textbook. The words are grouped according to the vowel sounds they contain.

ad	et	bis	hoc	dum
clam	mel	hic	mox	sub
nam	sex	id	ob	sum
pars	be´ne	is	quod	tum
iam	ce´ler	vir	ho´nor	urbs
al´ba	de´cem	dissi´milis	bōs	cul´tus
ar´ma	ec´ce	i´bi	nōs	cur´rus
bar´bara	le´gere	ig´nis	Ō	sum´mus
ca´sa	rever´tere	in´quit	sōl	tu´us
mag´na	sem´per	ni´hil	vōx	vul´nus
Lār	gēns	sī	cō´gō	plūs
pāx	plēbs	dī´vīsī	dō´nō	tū
trāns	spēs	dī´xī	nōs´cō	cursū´rus
ā´la	trēs	mī´sī	pō´nō	dū´rus
clā´ra	vēr	vī´cī	prōpō´nō	flūxus
fā´ma	crē´dere	vī´dī	co´lō	futū´rus
Fā´ta	dēbē´re	bi´bī	con´vocō	lū´dus
grā´ta	exercē´re	cī´vis	ho´mō	mū´nus
parā´ta	merē´re	fī´nis	oc´tō	nūl´lus
quā´rē	tenē´re	vīgin´tī	sol´vō	ū´nus

B **English derivatives of Latin** An English derivative is often easy to recognize because its spelling differs little or not at all from its Latin source, as in the following examples.

1. A light-blue stone often used in jewelry takes its name from the Latin word for *sea water.* Name it.

_____

2. Some people who live in seclusion, either by choice or from necessity, have a limited outlook on life. What English adjective, derived from the Latin word for *island,* describes this restricted perspective?

_____

Sometimes an English derivative differs greatly in spelling from its Latin source. In such instances, the shared meaning may still be quite clear.

3. Explain, if you can, how the meaning of the English word *savage* is related to the Latin word **silva.**

_____

4. Explain how the Latin word **via** is related in meaning to the English word *voyager.*

_____

Many proper nouns (names) in Latin have survived in English derivatives. Here is an example.

5. What word describes the type of a long verse or prose narrative dealing with adventure and love? (Hint: some of the most familiar examples of this literary form were written in French, Italian, and Spanish.)

_____

 Nouns in Latin and English Let's cover some basic terms you'll need to know. Begin by underlining each of the nouns in the following sentences.

1. A *noun* is the name of a person, place, thing, or idea.
2. In Latin, the *ending* of a noun can be variously spelled to express its *number* and its *case.*
3. The word *case* refers to a noun's grammatical function in a particular context.
4. The subject of a Latin sentence, for example, is expressed in the nominative case.
5. A group of nouns that share a set of similar endings is known as a declension.

Did you find twenty-five nouns?

 Noun functions: subject and predicate nominative In the following sentences, underline each noun used as a subject or as a predicate nominative. Do not include nouns that immediately follow a preposition (*of, by, for,* etc.), for these can never be subjects or predicate nominatives.

1. Twenty-five hundred years ago, Rome was an insignificant settlement on the Tiber River.
2. By the second century A.D., this city was the center of an empire.
3. The language of the Romans was Latin.
4. Spanish, Portuguese, French, Italian, and Romanian are the living descendants of the Latin spoken in ancient Rome.
5. Many English words are either derivatives or direct borrowings from Latin.

E **Latin to English translation** Translate each sentence.

1. Corsica est īnsula.

_____

2. Corsica et Melita sunt īnsulae.

_____

3. Nova Scotia paenīnsula est.

_____

4. Flōrida et Baia California paenīnsulae sunt.

_____

5. Īnsula Iaponia* et paenīnsula Korea* in Asiā sunt.

_____

*Iaponia and Korea are nouns in apposition to the subjects īnsula and paenīnsula. Do not include the word *of* in translating them.

6. Sunt* silvae in Germāniā.

_____

*It is sometimes best to start your translation with *there*, especially when the linking verb appears first in a Latin sentence.

7. In Scandinaviā tundra* est**.

_____

*Tundra is a level, treeless plain found in Arctic regions.
**See note on sentence 6 above.

8. Trōia* nōn in Āfricā sed in Asiā est.

_____

*This ancient city was the site of a famous war.

9. Hispānia in Eurōpā est. Nicaragua et Costa Rica in Latīnā Americā sunt.

_____

10. Estne* aqua in Saharā? Estne* in Canadā aqua?

_____

*The final letters **-ne** are simply the sign of a question. They do not change the meaning of the word on which they appear. You will learn more about this in a future lesson.

LESSON II

SICILIA

 Pronunciation: Special Sounds The following Latin words are grouped according to the diphthong, double vowel, and/or special consonant sound (*c, g, i,* and *v*) they contain. Before you use them for further pronunciation practice, be sure to read the pronunciation guide on pages 9–11 in the Introduction section of your textbook.

ae´quus	iō	a´ger
aes´tās	ia´ciō	di´gitus
par´vae	iū´dicō	in´teger
puel´lae		neglegen´tia
lau´dō	mai´or	amphitheā´trum
pau´cī	pei´or	philoso´phia
Poeni´cia	accē´dō	āver´tō
Poe´nī	acci´piō	a´vus
	audā´cia	captī´vus
cui	benefi´cium	cōnser´vō
huic	cer´tus	mo´veō
	cir´cus	nā´vis
	disci´pulus	
	do´ceō	

 Vocabulary Complete each sentence with an English word drawn from your Latin vocabulary.

1. We sent the letter _____ *(by way of)* the quickest route.

2. Because Charlie worked steadily, he was awarded a _____ *(incentive to do more good work).*

3. Those who apply for a scholarship must submit a _____ *(biography).*

4. Because she is a diver, she is said to love _____*tic* sports.

5. On the maps of early explorers an unknown area was often labeled _____ *incognita.*

6. One who watches an event is a _____*tor.*

Noun functions: subject and predicate nominative In the following sentences, underline each noun used as a subject or as a predicate nominative.

1. In Greek mythology, Zeus was the ruler of gods and men.

2. The Roman name of this god was Jupiter.

3. The eagle and the thunderbolt were symbols of his power.

4. Juno, his wife, was the goddess of marriage and the queen of heaven.

5. The home of these deities was Mount Olympus.

 Note the prepositional phrases in these sentences. *Prepositions* are words such as *of, in, by, from,* etc. The nouns that closely follow a preposition are called *objects of a preposition*. Objects of prepositions can never be predicate nominatives or subjects.

D **Sentence analysis** In each sentence, identify:

   a. the *subject* (thing(s) or person(s) spoken about)

   b. the *predicate* (statement)

   c. the *verb* (part of the predicate that is the main action)

   d. the *verb complement* (remaining part of the predicate, including nouns, adjectives, or prepositional phrases)

1. Cythera est īnsula.

   A. SUBJECT(S) _____

   B. PREDICATE _____

   C. VERB _____

   D. COMPLEMENT _____

2. Macedonia et Thrācia sunt magnae terrae in Eurōpā.

   A. SUBJECT(S) _____

   B. PREDICATE _____

   C. VERB _____

   D. COMPLEMENT _____

3. Familiae nōn magnae sunt sed vīta est bona in Siciliā.

   A. SUBJECT(S) _____

   B. PREDICATE(S) _____

   C. VERB(S) _____

   D. COMPLEMENTS _____

Both predicate nouns and predicate adjectives are called subject complements because they complete the linking verb's description of a subject. What case does Latin use to express subject complements?

_____

_____

E **Subject complements** Underline the subject complement in each of the following sentences. Translate these words in the spaces provided. Mark each as a predicate noun or predicate adjective.

Nota•Bene   A *subject complement* may contain both a noun and an adjective. When this occurs, the predicate adjective does not directly refer to the subject; it describes the predicate noun.

1. Euboea est īnsula.

_____

2. Phrygia et Scythia sunt terrae in Asiā.

_____

3. Iūturna et Lāra nymphae sunt.

_____

4. Aqua in Arethūsā bona est.

_____

5. Via Aemilia et Via Aurēlia longae viae sunt.

_____

F **Subject, predicate nouns and adjectives, prepositional phrases** Underline once the subject noun in each sentence. Circle the prepositional phrases. Then list the predicate nouns and predicate adjectives that are the subject complements.

1. Many roads built in the days of the ancient Romans are still functional.

_____

2. These hard-surfaced highways are engineering marvels.

_____

3. Their beds are deep, and their courses are very direct.

_____

4. The Appian Way, to cite an example, was and still is a very busy road in Rome today.

_____

5. It was the gift of Appius Claudius to the Roman people.

_____

G **Latin to English translation** The following sentences tell a story about the illustration. Translate each sentence. Remember to add the articles *the* or *a* when needed.

Cornēlia   *Iūlia*

Anna

Paula

1. Anna est parva.

   _____

   _____

   _____

2. Est puella parva.

   _____

   _____

   _____

3. Cornēlia magna puella est.

   _____

4. Anna et Paula sunt parvae puellae.

   _____

5. Magnae puellae sunt Cornēlia et Iūlia.

   _____

6. Magnae puellae parvās puellās portant.

   _____

7. Parvae puellae pūpās *(dolls)* amant.

   _____

8. Estne Iūlia parva?

   _____

9. Estne Paula magna?

   _____

10. Portantne Cornēlia et Iūlia pūpās?

   _____

Name _____ Date _____

H **Roman numerals** Roman numerals observe a few basic principles with which you are probably familiar. Let's review.

1. Certain letters are numerals.   M = _____

2. Other quantities can be expressed by   CCC = _____
   adding numerals of equal value or by adding
   a numeral of smaller value to a greater one.   LV = _____

3. When a numeral of smaller value   XL = _____
   is placed in front of a larger one, its
   value is subtracted from the larger
   numeral.

4. To express some numbers, you must   XXIV = _____
   combine these last two principles.

Add the Arabic numbers that you have   A = [   ]
supplied up to now.

Now convert the Roman numeral DCLXVI   B = [   ]
and place it in box B. Subtract it from the
total in box A to give an answer in box C.   C = [   ]

Your answer is a date of special significance in Roman history. What happened in this year B.C.? (Hint: Romulus and Remus accomplished this.)

_____

Name _____ Date _____

1 **Roman numerals** Just for fun, can you find the Roman numerals that are hidden in the following proper nouns? Identify these people and places using an encyclopedia as you search their names for letters that are also numerals.

EXEMPLĪ GRĀTIĀ

Vergil   <u>V</u>   <u>5</u>   (and)   <u>I L</u>   <u>49</u>

1. Cicero   __ __ __   _____

2. Livy   __ __ __   _____

3. Graecia   __ __   _____

4. Pompeiī   __   _____

   __ __   _____

5. Vesuvius   __   _____

   __ __   _____

6. Poseidon   __ __   _____

7. Sīlēnus   __ __   _____

8. Mīnōs   __ __   _____

9. Eurydicē   __ __   _____

10. Ulixēs   __ __ __   _____

LESSON III

ANNA ET RĀNA

A **Verbs: number** Indicate whether each pronoun is singular, plural, or both.

		SINGULAR	PLURAL
1.	we	_____	_____
2.	she	_____	_____
3.	you	_____	_____
4.	they	_____	_____
5.	I	_____	_____

Indicate whether each Latin inflection (personal ending) is singular or plural.

		SINGULAR	PLURAL
6.	-t	_____	_____
7.	-ō	_____	_____
8.	-tis	_____	_____
9.	-s	_____	_____
10.	-mus	_____	_____

Indicate whether each verb is singular or plural. Then write its meaning in the space provided.

		SINGULAR	PLURAL	MEANING
11.	spec´tat	_____	_____	_____
12.	amā´mus	_____	_____	_____
13.	pa´rās	_____	_____	_____
14.	labōrā´tis	_____	_____	_____
15.	por´tō	_____	_____	_____

Name _____ Date _____

B **Verbs: person** Identify the person of each verb. Then give its meaning.

	FIRST	SECOND	THIRD	MEANING
1. labō´rō	_____	_____	_____	_____
2. portā´tis	_____	_____	_____	_____
3. parā´mus	_____	_____	_____	_____
4. a´mant	_____	_____	_____	_____
5. spec´tō	_____	_____	_____	_____
6. pa´rat	_____	_____	_____	_____
7. labō´rās	_____	_____	_____	_____
8. por´tat	_____	_____	_____	_____
9. spec´tant	_____	_____	_____	_____
10. a´mās	_____	_____	_____	_____

C **Verbs: person and number** Identify both the person and number of each verb.

	FIRST	SECOND	THIRD	SINGULAR	PLURAL
1. spectā´tis	_____	_____	_____	_____	_____
2. labōrā´mus	_____	_____	_____	_____	_____
3. a´mō	_____	_____	_____	_____	_____
4. pa´rant	_____	_____	_____	_____	_____
5. por´tās	_____	_____	_____	_____	_____

Name _____ Date _____

D **Summary of verb concepts** Answer each question by circling the appropriate answer from each group.

1. Which of the following is not singular?

   a. labō´rās   **b.** pa´rō   **c.** portā´mus   **d.** spec´tat

2. Which of the following is not plural?

   a. a´mant   **b.** spec´tās   **c.** parā´tis   **d.** labōrā´mus

3. Which of the following is an infinitive?

   a. parā´mus   **b.** labōrā´tis   **c.** amā´re   **d.** spec´tō

4. Which of the following is a present stem?

   a. por´tō   **b.** por´tant   **c.** portā´re   **d.** por´tā-

5. Which of the following does not retain the stem vowel?

   a. labō´rō   **b.** labō´rās   **c.** labō´rant   **d.** labōrā´mus

E **Verb features in Latin** In each group, circle the three forms that share a common feature. Explain the reasons for your choices.

1. pa´rat   por´tō   a´mant   spec´tās

   _____

2. spec´tō   pa´rās   por´tō   labō´rō

   _____

3. labōrā´re   spectā´tis   parā´mus   a´mat

   _____

4. amā´mus   labō´rat   spec´tant   portā´tis

   _____

5. por´tat   a´mō   labō´rās   par´ā-

   _____

F **English to Latin translation: verbs** Translate the italicized words in each sentence.

EXEMPLĪ GRĀTIĀ In his forge beneath Mt. Aetna, Vulcan *is preparing* a shield.
            parat

1. He *works* on Sicily with his companions, the Cyclopes.

   _____

2. Vulcan: "Today we *are preparing* armor for a mighty warrior."

   _____

   _____

3. Venus, the warrior's mother, *is watching*.

   _____

4. Vulcan: "*Do* you *like* the shield?"

   _____

5. Venus: "I *like* it. It *is* strong and its designs *are* impressive."

   _____

6. The Cyclopes all *carry* the shield to the furnace.

   _____

7. Venus: "Tell me, Cyclopes, why *are* you (pl.) *watching* the fire so carefully?"

   _____

8. Cyclopes: "It takes much attention for us *to prepare* good armor."

   _____

9. Vulcan removes the shield from the fire and *carries* it to Venus.

   _____

10. Venus: "I am pleased. You and your companions *work* well."

   _____

Name _____ Date _____

LESSON IV

VIAE

 A **Direct object complements** Remember that direct objects, like predicate nouns and adjectives, are not part of a prepositional phrase. The action of a verb directly affects them and so, in English, they generally follow right after the verb. Use this information to locate five direct object nouns in the sentences below (label them D.O.)

> The emperor Augustus placed a golden milestone in the Roman Forum. It was known as the **Millārium Aureum.** From this column, part of which survives today, the Romans measured distances to other cities. Close to the marker, but older by far, was a famous road called the Sacra Via. It ran to the foot of the Capitoline Hill. Along this road the ancient Romans often drove animals toward a temple of Jupiter known as the **Capitolium.** There, at the chief shrine of their chief god, they offered both sacrifices and prayers.

 B **Declension of nouns and adjectives** As you know, the ending of a Latin noun and adjective tells you many important things.

- It indicates case (either nominative or accusative, for instance).
- It indicates a number (either singular or plural) of persons, places, things, or ideas.
- It is also a sign of gender.

1. Name the three genders of Latin nouns.

   _____ _____ _____

The nouns you learned in Lessons I through III use a specific set of case endings. Because they share those endings, we refer to them as a *declension*. The nouns you learned in the first three lessons are called *first declension* nouns. Lesson IV introduces a new group of nouns with a different set of endings. They are known as the *second declension*.

2. To which declension does **puella** belong?_____

3. To which declension does **servus** belong?_____

4. What do the endings **-a** and **-us** have in common?_____

   _____

5. What do the endings **-ās** and **-ōs** have in common?_____

   _____

6. In the sentence **Puella bona est,** what three things does the **-a** in **bona** tell you about the noun?

CASE _____

NUMBER _____

GENDER _____

7. If you translate *The cart is good* into Latin, should you use the same form of the adjective **(bona)?** Why or why not?

_____

8. What ending must the adjective have in this sentence *The cart is good*?

_____

C **Nouns of first/second declension: case and number** Answer the following.

1. Give the nominative plural of **terra.** _____

2. Give the accusative singular of **īnsula.** _____

3. Give the accusative plural of **via.** _____

4. Give the accusative singular of **carrus.** _____

5. Give the accusative plural of **equus.** _____

D **Summary of nouns** Circle the correct answer.

1. Which of the following is not nominative?

   a. carrī   **b.** fāma   **c.** equum   **d.** fortūnae

2. Which of the following is not accusative?

   a. familiam   **b.** servō   **c.** equōs   **d.** carrum

3. Which of the following could not be the subject in a Latin sentence?

   a. equus   **b.** īnsulās   **c.** via   **d.** silvae

4. Which of the following could not be the direct object in a Latin sentence?

   a. carrōs   **b.** vītam   **c.** aquās   **d.** servus

5. Which of the following could not be a subject complement?

   a. servum   **b.** agricola   **c.** terrae   **d.** equī

E **Agreement of nouns and adjectives** Remember that a Latin adjective must agree with the noun it describes in case, number, and gender. For the nouns and adjectives studied so far, this means that the spelling of the adjective's ending must match the ending of the noun.

Use the following eight forms to translate the word *great* in the story below. Be sure to determine the case, the number, the gender, and the declension of the noun that the adjective must describe; to tell its case, you must analyze how the noun is used in the sentence. Here are the adjective forms from which to choose.

	FIRST DECLENSION			SECOND DECLENSION	
	SINGULAR	PLURAL		SINGULAR	PLURAL
NOM.	magna	magnae	NOM.	magnus	magnī
ACC.	magnam	magnās	ACC.	magnum	magnōs

1. Ulysses was a *great* man. _____

2. His kingdom, Ithaca, was a *great* island. _____

3. Two *great* men named Achilles and Agamemnon were his companions in war.

_____

4. The *great* lands Greece and Troy fought in this war. _____

5. At Troy, the Greeks built a *great* horse. _____

6. For this idea, Ulysses gained *great* fame. _____

7. He and his comrades defeated *great* Trojan men such as Hector and Troilus.

_____

8. For their many adventures, we remember the *great* families of Greece and Troy.

_____

THE ROMAN WORLD

UNIT I
REVIEW

Derivatives Review   In the space provided at the right, identify the Latin source word for each English derivative listed to the left. Your answers will spell a well-known saying in English when read from top to bottom.

deviation   _ _ _ _

longevity   _ _ _ _ _ _

malaria   _ _ _ _

terrace   _ _ _ _

support   _ _ _

aquarium   _ _ _

duration   _ _ _ _

innovation   _ _ _ _ _

multiple   _ _ _ _

spectacle   _ _ _ _

infamy   _ _ _

laudable   _ _ _ _

revitalization   _ _ _

comparison   _ _ _ _

laboratory   _ _ _ _ _

amiability   _ _ _

magniloquence   _ _ _ _ _

equestrian   _ _ _ _

UNIT II

ROMAN INFLUENCE

LESSON V

RŌMA

 A **Vocabulary** The Latin adjective **clārus, clāra [clārum]** has two English meanings, *clear* and *famous*. Because of derivatives like *clarity,* it is easy to remember the first meaning. However, you will often need to use the second meaning. Translate the following sentences using the second meaning above.

1. Pēgasus erat equus clārus.

   _____

2. Cleopātra rēgīna clāra erat.

   _____

3. Tiberius et Gāius Gracchus erant Rōmānī clārī.

   _____

4. Parthia et Bactria terrae clārae erant.

   _____

 B **Coordinating and subordinating conjunctions** You have learned the three Latin conjunctions **et, sed,** and **quod.** These words are used to join words or groups of words having the same form and grammatical function. In the following sentences, circle each conjunction and underline the specific words that it connects. Hint: look for words that have the same ending and part of speech (e.g., nouns, adjectives, etc.).

1. Cassiopeia et Xenobia erant rēgīnae.

2. Cimbria *(the Netherlands)* est parva et plāna.

3. Rōma erat et est clāra.

4. Britannia nunc est parva sed nōn semper *(always)* erat.

5. Agricolae labōrant quod terram amant.

C **Genitive case** Lesson V introduces the *genitive* case. The exact English meaning of a Latin noun used in the genitive case is *of* plus the noun's meaning.

EXEMPLĪ GRĀTIĀ

viae	*of the road*	**servī**	*of the slave*
viārum	*of the roads*	**servōrum**	*of the slaves*

Note that no Latin word meaning *of* appears before the Latin word. In Latin, the word *of* is communicated by the genitive case endings alone.

1. Which two of the four case endings above is identical to the nominative plural endings?

_____

Notice that, of these four genitive endings, it is the plural endings that are easiest to identify. Translate these phrases using *of* or *s'* where possible.

2. fāma equōrum _____

3. vīta agricolārum _____

4. numerus rēginārum _____

5. cibus Rōmānōrum _____

The genitive singular is easy to recognize when it is used with a nominative singular. Translate these phrases using *of* or *'s*.

6. pūpa *(doll)* puellae _____

7. cibus servī _____

It is important to realize that genitive words are closely connected to the nouns they stand next to. This is especially clear in complete sentences.

Rēgīna Britanniae est clāra.   **Cibus servī bonus est.**

The queen of Britain is famous.   *The slave's food is good.*

Words in the genitive case can also appear next to nouns in the accusative case.

Rēgīnam Britanniae laudāmus.   **Cibum servī parō.**

We praise the queen of Britain.   *I get the slave's food.*

Translate the following examples of the above. Two translations may be possible.

8. numerus īnsulārum _____

9. fortūnam rēgīnae _____

D **Difficulties of the genitive case** Some difficulty arises when a genitive noun and a nominative noun with identical endings are used together.

EXEMPLĪ GRĀTIĀ

cūrae familiae **carrī servī**

Remember that in constructions like these, the second noun most often will be the genitive form. Common sense, however, will also help to reveal which of the two words have a genitive ending. *Families of the care* or *slaves of the cart* each make less sense than *cares of the family* and *carts of the slave*. Be careful to analyze endings before translating.

In each sentence, underline the subject and subject complement (predicate nominative). Circle the genitive words and then translate the sentence. (Note: **Aegyptus** and **Cyprus** are second declension nouns.)

1. Cibī Aegyptī erant multī et bonī.

_____

2. Equī Arabiae sunt clārī.

_____

3. Silvae Finlandiae magnae sunt.

_____

4. Viae Cyprī nōn longae sunt.

_____

5. Fortūnae Cleopātrae et Marcī Antonī erant malae.

_____

E **Case identification** Identify the case and number of each noun. More than one answer may be possible. Translate each word according to case and number in the space provided.

NOUNS	CASE	NUMBER	TRANSLATION
1. fōrmae	_____	_____	_____
2. numerum	_____	_____	_____
3. rēgīnārum	_____	_____	_____
4. cūrās	_____	_____	_____
5. cibōs	_____	_____	_____
6. carrī	_____	_____	_____
7. agricola	_____	_____	_____
8. vītam	_____	_____	_____
9. equus	_____	_____	_____
10. carrōrum	_____	_____	_____

LESSON VI

EURŌPA

 A The English word *to* can occur in very different constructions. It can be followed by a verb *(to sail)* or a noun *(to Greece)*.

1. Which of the two constructions named above is a prepositional phrase?

_____

2. What is the other construction called?

_____

In Latin, as in English, prepositions must have objects. These objects are nouns or pronouns, and in Latin these objects have special case endings, usually accusative. Each time you learn a preposition, the textbook will tell you which case ending to use with the objects of that preposition.

Ad, for instance, is always followed by an object with an accusative case ending.

EXEMPLĪ GRĀTIĀ

> **Ostia ad Rōmam est.**   **Ad Ostiam nāvigābimus.**

Translate these two sentences using the different meanings of **ad** you have learned.

3. _____

4. _____

 B So far, you have been using Latin verbs in the present tense. Although each present tense verb form may have various translations in English, it always refers to action that is going on *now*. **Parāmus,** for example, means:

> *we prepare*   *we do prepare*   *we are preparing*

In Latin, the *auxiliary* (or *helping*) verbs *do* and *are* are not expressed by separate words as they are in English, but they are contained in the verb **parāmus.**

The same concept applies to the future tense in Latin. You must translate Latin future tense forms with the English helping verbs *shall* and *will*.

Compare the following two forms and their translations.

> **laudās**   *you [do] praise*   **laudābis**   *you will praise*

1. What two parts of these Latin words are identical?

_____

2. What part of the future form is different?

_____

Separate the following pairs of verbs into their component parts as you have done above.

	COMMON STEM	COMMON ENDING	FUTURE TENSE SIGN
3. portat portābit	_____	_____	_____
4. spectāmus spectābimus	_____	_____	_____
5. parātis parābitis	_____	_____	_____
6. amant amābunt	_____	_____	_____

Note: The first person singular does not follow the pattern that you have identified here.

nāvig ō   **nāvigā b ō**

C **Present and future tense verb forms** Complete each exercise. Read each set of instructions carefully.

1. Change each verb from singular to plural, keeping the tense the same.
- **a.** amābis   *Amabitis*
- **b.** labōrat   *Laborant*
- **c.** nāvigō   *Navigamus*
- **d.** est   *Sunt*

2. Change each verb from plural to singular. Translate the new verb form.
- **a.** parāmus   *Parō*   *I prepare*
- **b.** spectātis   *Spectas*   *I look at*
- **c.** laudābunt   *Laudabit*   *he/she/it praise*
- **d.** parant   *Parat*   *He/she/it prepares*

3. Change each verb from the present to the future tense. Translate the new verb form.
- **a.** portāmus   *Portabimus*   *We will carry*
- **b.** parō   *Parabo*   *I will prepare*
- **c.** labōrās   *Laborabis*   *You will work*

4. Change each verb from the future tense to the present tense. Translate the new verb form.
- **a.** laudābō   *Laudo*   *I praise*
- **b.** labōrābunt   *Laborant*   *They work*
- **c.** spectābimus   *Spectamus*   *We watch*

D **English to Latin translation: verbs** Using your knowledge of the present and future tenses, translate the italicized verbs in each sentence. Be sure to make each verb agree with its subject by choosing the appropriate personal ending.

1. Jason *is preparing to sail* to Colchis.

   _____

2. In that faraway land, *there is* a golden fleece that he must obtain for the king of Thessaly.

   _____

3. *He will sail* from Greece with many heroes.

   _____

4. Among his companions are Hercules and the Gemini.*

   _____

   *Can you name these famous twins?

5. Medea, the princess of Colchis, *will look at* Jason and *(will) praise* him.

   _____

6. Medea will say: "Because *I love* you, *I will prepare* a magic potion."

   _____

7. She will tell Jason: "Beware! A fearsome dragon *watches* the golden fleece."

   _____

8. She will promise: "If you use my potion, however, *you will* safely *get/obtain* the treasure."

   _____

9. Jason *will carry* the potion with him and will overcome the dragon.

   _____

10. After they carry* the fleece aboard the Argo, Medea and Jason *will sail* with it to Greece.

    _____

    *Note: *carry* in this sentence would not be correctly translated with the present tense. Can you tell why not?

LESSON VII

COLUMBUS

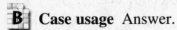 **A** **Case forms** Circle the correct answer to each of the following questions.

1. Which of the following is not nominative?

   a. nautīs   **b.** agricola   **c.** equus   **d.** viae

2. Which is not genitive?

   a. silvārum   **b.** carrī   **c.** familiae   **d.** cūrīs

3. Which is not dative?

   a. undīs   **b.** servō   **c.** rēgīnae   **d.** īnsulam

4. Which cannot be singular?

   a. terram   **b.** cibum   **c.** litterās   **d.** cōpiā

5. Which cannot be plural?

   a. pecūniās   **b.** praeda   **c.** numerōs   **d.** amīcōrum

B **Case usage** Answer.

1. For what purposes do Latin words have cases?

   _____

2. What are the names of the cases that use the following pairs of endings?

   us   ī   _____   a   ae

   ī   ōrum   _____   ae   ārum

   um   ōs   _____   am   ās

3. Which case is used to express the following?

   a. possession _____

   b. subjects _____

   c. predicate nouns and adjectives _____

   d. direct objects _____

4. Do any of the preceding endings appear in both the first and second declensions?

   _____

5. Write down the endings that are used for more than one case. Then identify the case and number that each ending may signify.

ENDING	CASE AND NUMBER	CASE AND NUMBER
_____ :	_____	_____
_____ :	_____	_____

Lesson VII introduces the *dative* case. As you can see, one of the dative endings (**-ae**) is the same as two other case endings you already know.

The noun **rēgīnae,** for example, can be used three ways.

Elizabetha et Victōria erant clārae Britannae rēgīnae.

1. In this sentence, **rēgīnae** means _____ and is _____ case.

Cūrae Elizabethae Rēgīnae multae erant.

2. In this sentence, **rēgīnae** means _____ and is _____ case.

(One of Elizabeth's greatest concerns was a war with Spain.)

Nauta rēgīnae victōriam nūntiat.

3. In this sentence, **rēgīnae** is dative case and therefore means _____.

(The *sailor* in the sentence above is Sir Francis Drake.)

Since Latin word order is highly flexible and because certain endings can signal more than one case, consider the following:

• If a noun ending in **-ae** is nominative plural, its verb must be plural to agree with it.

• If it is genitive, you should be able to translate it as such by relating it to another noun nearby.

• The third use of **-ae** (the dative case) is recognized as a dative ending primarily by the verb with which it appears. Verbs that express the idea of *giving, showing, telling,* or *entrusting* often require an indirect object. This is expressed in English by the preposition *to* and in Latin by the dative case (give *to*, show *to*, etc.).

Notice, furthermore, that the dative singular ending of second declension nouns is distinctive.

Servus Marcī equō cibum dōnat.

The dative plural endings (**-īs**) are also distinct from those of the other three cases you have learned. Take note, however: this is the only ending you know that is shared by both declensions.

      to the girls   =   **puellīs**

      to the friends =   **amīcīs**

 D **Dative case** In the following passage, circle each word that would be dative in Latin. Underline the phrases that would require the Latin preposition **ad** plus an object in the accusative case. Remember that the dative case word in Latin is the indirect object in English.

Jupiter, the ruler of gods and men, entrusted many duties to his son, the messenger Mercury. As a courier, Mercury sped to all parts of the world with urgent messages. He announced to mortal men the counsels of Olympus. In the course of his travels, he showed his staff to the winds, and they parted for him.

As patron of commerce and travel, Mercury gave his blessing to merchants and came to the aid of pilgrims. He even conducted the spirits of the dead to the Underworld. It was Mercury who made the first lyre and presented it to his brother Apollo. He also gave Hercules a sword, Perseus a helmet, and Ulysses a magic herb. It is easy to recognize Mercury in a museum; he wears a wide-brimmed hat and carries a staff. There are wings not only on the hat and the staff, which is called the **caduceus,** but also on his sandals.

 E **English to Latin translation** Use the words provided below to create and translate your own Latin sentences. First, complete the chart with the specific Latin word forms requested. Next, for each sentence, select a subject, an indirect object, and a direct object. Be sure the subject agrees with the verb in number. Finally, translate the sentence in the space provided. Although there may be many possible combinations, some will make more sense than others.

NOMINATIVE		ACCUSATIVE	
farmer	_____	money	_____
slaves	_____	food	_____
girls	_____	letter	_____
queen	_____	victories	_____
DATIVE		loot	_____
friend	_____	carts	_____
sailor	_____	road	_____
horses	_____		
Romans	_____		

Name _____ Date _____

1. _____   _____
      (subject)   (indirect object)

_____ dōnat.
      (direct object)

Translation: _____

2. _____   _____
      (subject)   (indirect object)

_____ mandat.
      (direct object)

Translation: _____

3. _____   _____
      (subject)   (indirect object)

_____ mōnstrant.
      (direct object)

Translation: _____

4. _____   _____
      (subject)   (indirect object)

_____ nūntiant.
      (direct object)

Translation: _____

LESSON VIII

GALLIA

A **Ablative case: place where** This lesson introduces an important use of the *ablative* case. You may already be familiar with the *ablative of place where* construction, which frequently appears with the preposition *in*.

> **Rōma est in Italiā.**

The phrase **in Italiā** answers the question *where?* in this sentence. How does its case ending differ in spelling from that of **Rōma?**

_____

Your textbook explains that the ablative case is used to distinguish the objects of certain prepositions (such as *in*). You will learn more about this preposition later. At this point, however, to practice with the new case endings, translate the following phrases.

1. in Libya _____
2. in Damascus _____
3. in the waves _____
4. in the wagons _____

B **Ablative case: means by which** This use of the ablative case with the preposition *in* is only one of many uses of the ablative. You will often encounter a word or a phrase in the ablative case which is not the object of any preposition. In such a construction, the ablative endings themselves, like those of the dative and genitive cases, supply the prepositions required for English translation. The ablative case is often used, for example, to indicate *means*. Whenever you identify this type of ablative, translate it with the English words *by* or *with*.

Translate each noun in the ablative case.

1. aquā _____
2. cibō _____
3. pecūniā _____
4. carrō _____
5. fortūnā _____

Use the five preceding Latin words to answer each question.

6. How do you fill a cornucopia *(horn of plenty)?* _____

7. How do you pay for a football ticket? _____

8. How do you take a hayride? _____

9. How do you resuscitate a drooping flower? _____

10. How do you win the flip of a coin for a kickoff? _____

How would you translate each ablative phrase?

11. undīs magnīs _____

12. memoriīs bonīs _____

13. multīs victōriīs _____

14. parvīs litterīs _____

15. quattuor equīs* _____

    *Quattuor means *four.* Like most Latin numbers, it cannot be declined. It agrees with any plural form of a Latin noun, regardless of the noun's case ending.

Use the Latin phrases from questions 11–15 to answer each of the following questions.

16. How does a team become qualified for the playoffs? _____

17. How are special moments preserved? _____

18. How were Roman chariots pulled? _____

19. How is a wedding ring engraved? _____

20. How is a surfboard propelled? _____

C **English to Latin translation: ablatives** In the following story, certain words are used to express *means.* Others are used as objects of the preposition *in.* The correct Latin form of the nouns in each instance will be ablative. Translate the italicized phrases.

Remember: the *ablative* of *means* never uses a Latin preposition. When the word *in* refers to a place, however, it must be expressed with its Latin cognate, **in.**

  1–2. Many years ago *in Italy,* King Numitor was driven from the throne of Alba Longa *by the great injustice* of his brother Amulius.

      _____

      _____

  3. Numitor's only daughter, the princess Rhea Silvia, was forced to live *in the household** of the Vestal Virgins.

      _____

    *Use the noun **familia** here. This word refers not only to biological families, but to all the people living under one roof.

4. One day, as she was drawing water *in the forest,* the god Mars was attracted to her and made her the mother of twins named Romulus and Remus.

_____

5. The outraged Amulius murdered his niece and afflicted her sons *with harsh penalties.*

_____

6–7. He instructed a loyal slave of the princess to bring the two infants to the river Tiber *by horse* or *wagon* and drown them.

_____

_____

8. He set both boys in a watertight basket and put it *in the waters* of the Tiber River.

_____

9–10. *With (its) small waves* the river cast the twins ashore *on land* that would later be known as the Roman Forum.

_____

_____

11. Today a famous fig tree stands on that spot and commemorates the story of Romulus and Remus *with (its) pleasing shape.*

_____

LESSON IX

CORNĒLIA ET NAUTA

 Case usage The following sentences have been composed to show you all five cases at work together. Notice that the word order of each example preserves the regular sequence of singular forms (nominative, genitive, dative, etc.).

Fīlia	agricolae	nautae	viam	ferulā	mōnstrat.	
The daughter	of the farmer	to the sailor	a road	with her staff	points out	
Servus	**equō**	**Marcī**	**cibum**	**in**	**saccō**	**dōnat.**
The servant	to the horse	of Marcus	food	in	a sack	gives

 Case usage Now that you know all five case endings, you can correctly use the noun *Rome* (**Rōma**) in each sentence. Write down the case and number needed on the left side and the correct spelling of **Rōma** on the right.

1. By many generations of admirers, *Rome* has been called the **urbs aeterna.**

_____   _____

2. Though two thousand years have elapsed, the glory *of Rome* remains undimmed.

_____   _____

3. The presence of the past gives *Rome* an atmosphere entirely its own.

_____   _____

4. For this reason, people from all parts of the world visit *Rome* each year.

_____   _____

5. In Rome they see and praise the traces of an ancient civilization.

_____   _____

Name _____ Date _____

You can also translate plural nouns in all five cases. In sentences 6–10, identify the case needed on the left; then provide the correct plural form of the word **prōvincia** on the right.

6. Spain and France were once *provinces* of Rome.

_____   _____

7. The people *of* these former *provinces* still speak a Roman language.

_____   _____

8. In addition to this common tongue, Rome gave its *provinces* many aqueducts, buildings and roads, several of which are still in use.

_____   _____

9. Classicists, therefore, research not only Rome, but its *provinces* as well.

_____   _____

10. In some instances, the ancient structures are better preserved *in* these *provinces* than in Rome itself.

_____   _____

Adjective - noun agreement: masculine nouns of the first declension You have learned that adjectives agree in case, number, and gender with the nouns that they modify. This agreement, in most instances, appears as a repetition of the same case ending.

EXEMPLĪ GRĀTIĀ

    Fīlia grāta est.   **Servus grātus est.**

Sometimes, however, the endings required by the rules of agreement will not be exactly the same (e.g., **nauta bonus**). You have learned only two nouns that illustrate this unusual kind of agreement.

    agricola   *farmer*   **nauta**   *sailor*

1. To what declension do these nouns belong?

_____

2. What gender are most of the nouns in this declension?

_____

3. But what gender are **agricola** and **nauta?**

_____

Notice the use of adjectives in the following sentences. What is unusual about the italicized examples?

    Cincinnatus erat clārus.   **Mīsēnus et Palinūrus erant clārī.**

    Erat clārus Rōmānus.   **Erant clārī Troiānī.**

The adjectives **clārus** and **clārī** use second declension endings to agree with the first declension nouns **agricola** and **nautae.**

Later in your textbook you will learn one other word, **poēta,** which belongs to the first declension but is masculine in gender.

Clārum poētam Homērum laudāmus.   *We praise the famous poet Homer.*

Translate the italicized parts of each sentence. Be sure to consider whether a singular or plural case ending is needed.

4. In ancient times, the work *of a great poet* was always dedicated to one of the Muses.

_____

5. Venus assisted *the Trojan sailors.*

_____

6. Apollo gave no laurels *to a bad poet.*

_____

7. Scylla and Charybdis caused the deaths *of many sailors.*

_____

8. Ceres presented seed-corn *to the grateful farmers.**

_____

*Notice that, in this instance, the adjective and noun have the same ending.

D **Indicative vs. imperative** You now know many Latin verbs and can conjugate them in both the present and future tenses. With the indicative mood of these verbs, you can make statements and ask questions. In English, the subjects of statements and questions are expressed by nouns or pronouns. In Latin, as you have seen, subjects are often expressed simply by the personal endings of verbs.

Not every verb in Latin or English, however, appears with an expressed subject.

EXEMPLĪ GRĀTIĀ

Labōrā!   *Work!*

In English as well as in Latin, such commands are referred to as *imperatives*. The understood subject of an imperative verb is always the pronoun *you.* An imperative sentence, consequently, expresses an order or a direction of some kind.

This understood subject can obviously be either singular or plural. There are, therefore, two forms of the present imperative. To speak in this mood to a singular person, Latin simply uses the present stem.

Labōrā, fīlia!   *Work, daughter!*

The subject in this example is still the pronoun *you.* The noun of address (**fīlia**—vocative case) simply tells us that the subject is singular.

Plural imperatives echo the ending **-tis** by adding **-te** to the stem.

Labōrāte, fīliae!   *Work, daughters!*

Use the information to complete the following chart. Note that there is only one English translation for both the singular and plural imperatives.

INFINITIVE	PRESENT STEM/ IMPERATIVE SINGULAR	IMPERATIVE PLURAL	TRANSLATION
amāre	_____	_____	_____
_____	nāvigā	_____	_____
_____	_____	parāte	_____
_____	_____	_____	Watch!

ROMAN INFLUENCE

 Glimpses of Roman life: the Eternal City In Unit II, you have read about many features of the Eternal City. Now, on the map below, you can put it all into perspective. Consult an encyclopedia or a classical atlas for help if necessary.

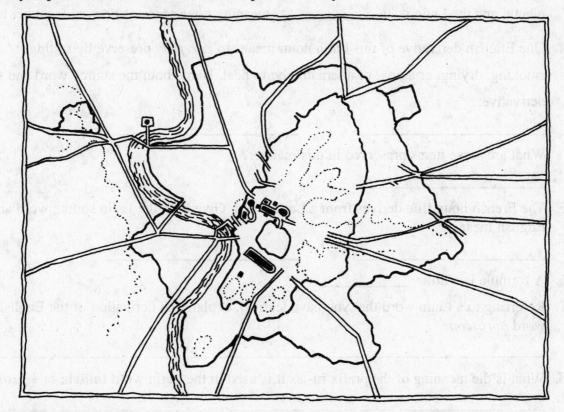

Label the following:

A. The Aurelian Wall

B. The Aventine Hill

C. The Caelian Hill

D. The Campus Martius

E. The Capitoline Hill

F. The Circus Maximus

G. The Coliseum

H. The Esquiline Hill

I. The Forum

J. The Ianiculum

K. The Palatine Hill

L. The Pantheon

M. The Quirinal Hill

N. The Sacra Via

O. The Servian Wall

P. The Tiber River

Q. The Vatican

R. The Via Appia

S. The Via Flaminia

T. The Viminal Hill

B **Vocabulary and derivatives review** Complete the following using vocabulary words studied in this unit.

1. A person who offers, or is called upon, to advise a court about legal matters is called a/an

   __ __ __ __ __ __ **curiae,** or literally, *a friend* of the court.

2. Ambrosia was the __ __ __ __ __ of the Olympian gods.

3. The Roman goddess Ops was the wife of Saturn. She was worshipped as the goddess of

   plenty, and the Latin noun __ __ __ __ __, meaning *abundance,* is derived from her name.

4. One English derivative of this Latin noun means to *carefully* preserve by salting,

   smoking, drying, or aging, or alternatively, to heal. Name both the source word and the

   derivative.

   _____   _____

   What are some items preserved in this manner?

   _____

5. The French noun **fille** derives from a Latin word. Give both the Latin source word and its
   English meaning.

   _____   _____

6. A formula is a little _____.

7. Referring to a Latin word that you have learned, explain the derivation of the English
   word *horoscope.*

   _____

8. What is the meaning of the prefix **in-** as it is used in the Latin word **iniūria** or *injustice?*

   _____

9. The English word *illiterate* means unlettered, or _____

10. Separate the English word *illiterate* into a prefix, a root, and a suffix.

    _____

11. What is meant by the phrase, *from time immemorial?*

    _____

12. What are the prefix, root, and suffix of *immemorial?*

    _____

13. Based on your analysis of the last three words (**iniūria,** *illiterate,* and *immemorial*) list
    three prefixes found in both Latin and English that sometimes share a common meaning.
    What is the common meaning of these prefixes?

    PREFIXES   **MEANING**

    _____, _____, _____   _____

Name _____ Date _____

14. What was the name of the first U.S. Navy submarine to be powered by atomic energy? From what Latin noun is its name derived?

_____

15. What is *numerology* and how does it differ from mathematics?

_____

16. What English adjectives are good synonyms for the word *impecunious?*

_____

17. Which letter of the Latin noun **poena** is not found in that word's most common derivatives? Write at least two of these derivatives and underline the slightly altered spelling of the root.

_____

18. By what means does a *predatory* animal live? Write the Latin word.

_____

19. How is the English word *provincial* an antonym of *sophisticated* or *worldly wise?*

_____

20. __ __ __ __ __ is the Latin word for the type of contest in which Muhammad Ali and Sugar Ray Leonard were champions.

21. The capital of Saskatchewan, Canada, is __ __ __ __ __ __, meaning *queen.*

22. In physics, the motion of light or sound is referred to as __ __ __ulation.

23. What Latin noun is the name of an Australian state, an African lake, and a one-time British queen?

_____

UNIT III

ROMANS AT HOME AND ABROAD

LESSON X

LINGUA LATĪNA

A Answer.

1. Which principal part of a Latin verb is the present active infinitive?

    a. first   **(b)** second   **c.** third   **d.** fourth

Portāre and **docēre** are infinitives of the first and second conjugations.

Portō means *I carry*.

2. Translate **portāre**.   To carry

Doceō means *I teach*.

3. Translate **docēre**.   To teach

Notice how the endings of the infinitive forms resemble one another. Notice also that the English translation of an infinitive is the same for verbs of both conjugations.

Translate.

4. dōnāre   to give

5. habēre   to have

6. servāre   to serve

7. terrēre   _____

B Give the Latin form of each English phrase.

1. we are teaching   docemus

2. you *(sing.)* teach   doces

3. I shall teach   docēo

4. you *(pl.)* are teaching   docetis

5. they will teach   docaunt

Give English translations for each of the following Latin verbs.

6. docēbit   _____

7. docent   _____

8. docēbitis   _____

9. doceō   _____

10. docet   _____

C The following list contains verbs of both the first and second conjugations. Circle the stem vowel in each form, and then translate each verb into English.

1. augētis   _____

2. parābitis   _____

3. laudat   _____

4. habet   _____

5. amāmus   _____

6. terrēbimus   _____

7. incitant   _____

8. augēbō   _____

9. labōrābis   _____

10. docēs   _____

D Let's review further.

1. What is the imperative mood used to express?

_____

2. From what stem is it formed?

_____

3. What does **spectā,** the singular imperative of the first conjugation verb **spectō,** mean?

_____

4. What does **spectāte** mean?

_____

5. How do the two forms differ?

_____

_____

6. Give and translate the corresponding imperative forms of the second conjugation verb **augēo.**

IMPERATIVE	TRANSLATION
_____	_____
_____	_____

E **Verb forms** Circle the two verb forms from each group that have something in common. Explain why they are similar.

1. portāre   augēre   laudāre

_____

2. augē   portāte   terrēte

_____

3. laudā   terrē   habēt

_____

4. habēo   laudā   augeō

_____

5. doceō   docēre   docē

_____

F One more review.

1. The word *conjugation* refers to a group of _____ (part of speech).

2. To determine whether a verb belongs to the first or second conjugation, at which of its principal parts must you look?

_____

3. What is this form called? _____

5. What is the last letter of the present stem of a first conjugation verb? _____

6. What is the last letter of the present stem of a second conjugation verb? _____

LESSON XI

CAESAR IN BRITANNIĀ

A **Vocabulary** Complete each sentence using vocabulary learned in this lesson.

1. Knowledge of Latin roots will lead to an *augmentation* of your English vocabulary, which means _____.

2. One who acknowledges the gradual *increases* in bidding at a public sale is called a/an _____.

3. The primary connotation of *discipline* to most people is _____. According to the derivation of the word, however, a better definition of discipline would be _____.

4. When we go to a museum to see a special exhibit, a trained staff member called a *docent* _____ us about the works of art on display.

5. Public television often shows *documentary* films. Broadcasts of this nature should _____ the viewers.

6. Many of the personnel at the United Nations are *multilingual*. They speak _____ _____.

7. **Semper parātus,** which means _____ _____, is the motto of the U.S. Coast Guard.

8. *Vainglorious* boasts are empty of real _____.

9. A person who leaves a *gratuity,* or tip, expresses his or her _____ or may try to gain _____.

10. Things that are *visible* are able to be _____.

11. A person who is *thankful* or *welcoming* is _____.

12. Something that is *unimportant* or does not *matter* is _____.

B **Ablative of place where** Translate.

1. in the forest _____

2. on a horse _____

3. in the road _____

4. on the island _____

5. in the provinces _____

C **Ablative of place where** How may the preposition **in** be translated in the following phrases (*in, on,* or *either*)?

1. in aquā   **a.** in   **b.** on   **c.** either

2. in litterīs   **a.** in   **b.** on   **c.** either

3. in memoriā   **a.** in   **b.** on   **c.** either

4. in terrā   **a.** in   **b.** on   **c.** either

5. in vītā   **a.** in   **b.** on   **c.** either

D **Ablative of place where** Label the picture below with the Latin phrases from the two previous exercises. Only seven phrases will work.

LESSON XII

PUERĪ RŌMĀNĪ

 Verb tenses: present, future, perfect Circle the Latin verb ending from each group that is not related to the others. Explain your choice by selecting a reason from the list at the end of the exercise.

					REASON
1.	-istī	-istis	-it	-ī	_____
2.	-imus	-ērunt	-it	-istis	_____
3.	-ō	-mus	-ī	-nt	_____
4.	-s	-bit	-istī	-bitis	_____
5.	-it	-imus	-s	-ērunt	_____
6.	-bunt	-mus	-tis	-nt	_____
7.	-t	-bit	-tis	-bunt	_____
8.	-istis	-bō	-bimus	-bis	_____
9.	-mus	-bimus	-imus	-ī	_____
10.	-istis	-bitis	-istī	-tis	_____

REASONS

I. The other three endings are first person endings.

II. The other three endings are second person endings.

III. The other three endings are third person endings.

IV. The other three endings are singular.

V. The other three endings are plural.

VI. The other three endings are used to express the present tense.

VII. The other three endings are used to express the future tense.

VIII. The other three endings are used to express the perfect tense.

B **Perfect tense** The perfect tense of Latin verbs has three possible English translations. Match the Latin words in Column I with an appropriate translation in Column II.

COLUMN I   COLUMN II

1. _____ amavī   **a.** he did hold

2. _____ terruistī   **b.** you have taught

3. _____ mandāvit   **c.** I loved

4. _____ monstrāvimus   **d.** you have seen

5. _____ docuistis   **e.** they saw

6. _____ līberāvērunt   **f.** we have shown

7. _____ portāvistī   **g.** I did incite

8. _____ auxistis   **h.** he had

9. _____ habuit   **i.** you sailed

10. _____ probāvērunt   **j.** I have earned

11. _____ nāvigāvistis   **k.** you carried

12. _____ tenuit   **l.** they did remain

13. _____ meruī   **m.** he has entrusted

14. _____ labōrāvistī   **n.** we did see

15. _____ occupāvimus   **o.** you have scared

16. _____ mānsērunt   **p.** we seized

17. _____ incitāvī   **q.** you did labor

18. _____ vīdimus   **r.** they freed

19. _____ vīdistis   **s.** you did increase

20. _____ vīdērunt   **t.** they have approved

C **Principal parts and verb stems** Answer.

1. The first principal part of a Latin verb gives us the first person singular of which tense?

_____

2. The third principal part of a Latin verb gives us the first person singular of which tense?

_____

3. From which principal part of a verb is the present stem derived?

_____

4. Which letter(s) of the form mentioned in the preceding question is/are dropped to reveal the present stem?

_____

5. From which principal part of a verb is the perfect stem derived?

_____

6. Which letter(s) of the form mentioned above is/are dropped to reveal the perfect stem?

_____

7. With which of these stems (present or perfect) do we form the future tense of a verb?

_____

8. Which personal endings do those of the future tense more closely resemble—those of the present or those of the perfect tense?

_____

9. What part of the future tense endings is special to that tense?

_____

D **Verb tenses: present, future, perfect** Translate. Note that each set contains forms in three different tenses.

1. incitat   incitābit   incitāvit

_____   _____   _____

2. terrent   terrēbunt   terruērunt

_____   _____   _____

3. vidēs   videbis   vīdistī

_____   _____   _____

4. parātis   parābitis   parāvistis

_____   _____   _____

5. augeō   augēbō   auxī

_____   _____   _____

6. servāmus   servābimus   servāvimus

_____   _____   _____

LESSON XIII

SERVĪ

 A **Vocabulary** The three prepositions of place introduced in Lesson XIII are commonly used as prefixes in English. Consider, for example, the following verbs.

      abstract   **de**tract   **ex**tract

In a later lesson, you will learn the verb **trahō** *(draw, drag),* the source of the root that you see here. Although the meanings of these prefixes are similar, try to define each derivative as distinctly as possible.

1. abstract _____

2. detract _____

3. extract _____

You can further practice distinguishing among **ab, dē,** and **ex** with the following set of adjectives.

      abject   **de**jected   **ej**ected

(The root **iect-** means *cast.*)

Match each definition with one of the preceding examples.

4. cast out   _____

5. cast away   _____

6. cast down   _____

B **Case usage** Translate the italicized word in each sentence. Refer to the second declension case endings. Be sure to examine the context carefully before selecting a case form.

1. A Roman *slave* was often a prisoner of war taken captive in the course of foreign conquests. _____

2. Because of their backgrounds, many *slaves* from civilized lands were better educated than their Roman masters. _____

3. The life of a Roman *slave* was not always unpleasant. _____

4. The tasks of some household *slaves,* for instance, were very simple and easy to perform. _____

5. Sometimes a master would assign great responsibilities to a *slave.* _____

6. The Romans even gave their *slaves* allowances to show that they appreciated faithful service. _____

7. They often honored a loyal *slave* after years of service by setting him free or permitting him to purchase his freedom. _____

8. They admitted former *slaves* into society without prejudice. _____

9. A kind master could expect to receive continued allegiance from a freed *slave.*
_____

10. You will learn more about slaves in this book. _____

C **Case identifications** Tell whether each of the following nouns is nominative, vocative, or can be both.

1. Clāra _____

2. agricolae _____

3. Brūtus _____

4. serve _____

5. servī _____

6. Iūlius _____

7. Horātī* _____

8. patria _____

9. amīce _____

10. Aemilī** _____

* Horātius, Horātī, *m.*
** Aemilius. Aemilī, *m.*

D The vocative case identifies nouns of address in two contexts.
- With regular verbs (indicative mood)
  Amīce, spectō.
  Labōrātisne, amīci?
- With commands (imperative mood)
  Manē, socī.
  Sociī, pugnāte!

Translate the preceding Latin phrases.

1. _____

2. _____

3. _____

4. _____

E **Perfect tense** By now, you realize the importance of memorizing all the principal parts of every new verb. Here are some second conjugation verbs that you have learned so far. List the third principal part of each one, translate it, and obtain its perfect stem.

	THIRD PART	TRANSLATION	PERFECT STEM
1. augeō	_____	_____	_____
2. doceō	_____	_____	_____
3. habeō	_____	_____	_____
4. maneō	_____	_____	_____
5. mereō	_____	_____	_____
6. moveō	_____	_____	_____
7. teneō	_____	_____	_____
8. terreō	_____	_____	_____
9. videō	_____	_____	_____

For further practice, here are the principal parts of iubeō (order, bid), another verb of the second conjugation that you will use later in this book.

iubeō **iubēre** **iussī** **iussus**

Although a verb is new to you, you now know how to find its perfect stem and form its perfect tense. Add **iubeō** to the preceding list by copying its third principal part, translating it, and giving its perfect stem.

	THIRD PART	TRANSLATION	PERFECT STEM
10. iubeō	_____	_____	_____

11. How many of the stems above are like the perfect stem of **doceō?** _____

12. List the verbs that, by contrast, have perfect stems ending in a consonant.

_____

Notice that there is variation in the spelling of the perfect stems of second conjugation verbs. List the third principal part of each first conjugation verb, translate it, and give its perfect stem.

	THIRD PART	TRANSLATION	PERFECT STEM
13. dōnō			
14. labōrō			
15. laudō			
16. mōnstrō			
17. parō			
18. portō			
19. pugnō			
20. servō			
21. spectō			
22. vocō			

Notice that these stems do not display the same kind of variations that you saw among second conjugation verbs.

23. What is the common ending of these stems (13–22)? _____

24. What capital letter did the Romans use for both the *u* and the *v* sounds? _____

25. Use this information to make a generalization about the perfect stems of all first and most second conjugation verbs.

_____
_____

LESSON XIV

ARISTOTELĒS ET ALEXANDER

 Noun stems For each of the following nouns give, in Latin, the nominative singular, the genitive singular, and the stem that is common to both forms. Be sure that you do not include any portion of a case ending in these stems.

EXEMPLĪ GRĀTIĀ

	NOMINATIVE SINGULAR	GENITIVE SINGULAR	NOUN STEM
fame	**fāma**	**fāmae**	**fām-**
number	**numerus**	**numerī**	**numer-**
1. form	_____	_____	_____
2. hour	_____	_____	_____
3. victory	_____	_____	_____
4. prisoner	_____	_____	_____
5. food	_____	_____	_____

As your textbook points out, the new masculine nominative case words ending in **-er** and **-r** have precisely the same second declension endings as those that end in **-us.** The base of some of these words may change, however. Do you remember which ones change?

 **Nouns ending in -r** Give the nominative plural forms of each, and then translate.

	FORM	MEANING
1. ager plānus	_____	_____
2. puer grātus	_____	_____
3. cibus tuus	_____	_____
4. Rōmānus līber	_____	_____
5. vir bonus	_____	_____

When two nouns of different genders share a common base, it is sometimes hard to distinguish masculine from feminine. **Amīcīs,** for instance, could mean *to the (male) friends,* or *to the (female) friends.* In such instances, the Romans sometimes avoided ambiguity by using an alternative set of case endings for feminine words. Note the following.

NOMINATIVE SINGULAR	**deus**	**dea**	**fīlius**	**fīlia**
DATIVE AND ABLATIVE PLURAL	**deīs**	**deābus**	**fīliīs**	**fīliābus**

Using these forms, translate the italicized words in each of the following sentences.

6. Roman parents gave their *daughters* a name and a bulla when they were eight days old.

_____

7. Roman parents gave their *sons* a name and a bulla when they were nine days old.

_____

8. Sacrifices were made at the Capitolium to Jupiter as well as to the *goddesses* Juno and Minerva. _____

9. Other temples in ancient Rome were dedicated to the *gods* Mars, Saturn, and Apollo.

_____

Adjectives ending in -er: base changes Notice that certain adjectives resemble the nouns introduced in this lesson; they too may change their base. Give the feminine and neuter nominative singulars of the following words, and then translate.

MASCULINE	FEMININE	NEUTER	MEANING
1. līber	_____	_____	_____
2. noster	_____	_____	_____
3. sacer	_____	_____	_____

The genitive singular forms of these adjectives will have stems seen in the feminine and neuter forms.

4. Which one of the preceding words retains **-er** in its stem? _____

5. What are the stems of the other two adjectives? _____

LESSON XV

COLŌNĪ RŌMĀNĪ

 Vocabulary In Lesson IV you were introduced to the nouns **dominus** *(master)* and **domina** *(mistress)*. Although these nouns resemble one another, they clearly belong to different declensions. You have now learned another pair of nouns, **fīlius** and **fīlia,** which are similarly related in meaning and form. Other nouns that you know, such as **servus** and **magister,** also have feminine equivalents: e.g. **serva** *(slave girl, maid)* and **magistra.**

What are the Latin equivalents of the following?

1. a female settler _____

2. a female prisoner _____

3. a female friend _____

B **Grammer review:** *sum as linking verb* Answer.

1. What case is a noun or adjective that is linked to a subject by est or sunt?

_____

2. To which part of speech do the italicized words belong?

Corinna *serva* est.   Sextus est *servus.*   Corinna et Sextus sunt *servī.*

_____

3. To which part of speech do the italicized words belong?

Aqua est *clāra.*   Cibus *bonus* est.   Aqua et cibus *grātī* sunt.

_____

4. What kind of verbs do the preceding Latin sentences have?

_____

C **The verb** *sum* Answer.

1. What are the principal parts of the Latin verb *to be?*

_____   _____   _____

_____

2. The second principal part of this verb does not look like other infinitives you have learned, yet it is translated in the same way. What does it mean?

_____

3. What is the last letter of the first principal part of verbs that you have learned so far?

_____

4. What is the last letter of the first principal part of this verb? _____

5. What is the last letter of the third principal part of this verb? _____

6. Does it have the same ending as other perfect tense verbs? _____

7. This third principal part, being the perfect tense, can mean _____
   or _____

8. What portion of the fourth principal part is the stem? _____

 D **Dialogue: the verb** *sum* Translate the following dialogue.

1. DOMINUS: Vir līber sum.

   _____

2. DOMINA: Et lībera sum.

   _____

3. DOMINUS: Familia nostra nōn magna est.

   _____

4. DOMINA: Gratī sumus quod cūrae nostrae sunt parvae.

   _____

5. DOMINUS: Es puella bona, fīlia mea.

   _____

6. DOMINA: Et puer bonus es, mi* fīlī.

   _____

*The masculine vocative singular of the adjective **meus** is **mī.**

 E **Case usage** Translate only the italicized words in each sentence. Pay attention to case.

1. There are many inspiring monuments *in our country*.

   _____

2. Plymouth Rock, for instance, commemorates *the great courage* of the settlers who first
   came to this continent in search of personal liberties.

   _____

3. As a tribute to democracy, the people of France presented the Statue of Liberty to the *free men* of the United States.

_____

4. The *many boys* who have died for our country in foreign wars are honored by the Tomb of the Unknown Soldier.

_____

5. Arlington Cemetery, in which this monument stands, is a *sacred field*.

_____

 Prepositions: *ad* and *in,* **place to which** Circle the Latin words needed to translate the following phrases correctly. Remember that **ad** or **in** plus the accusative express *place to which.*

1. in the field	ad	in	agrum	agrō
2. to the field	ad	in	agrum	agrō
3. near the house	ad	in	casam	casā
4. in the house	ad	in	casam	casā
5. into the house	ad	in	casam	casā
6. to the house	ad	in	casam	casā
7. in the waves	ad	in	undās	undīs
8. into the waves	ad	in	undās	undīs
9. near the standard	ad	in	signum	signō
10. to the standard	ad	in	signum	signō

LESSON XVI

TRŌIA

A **Neuter nouns of the second declension** Answer.

1. What is the nominative singular case ending of a first declension noun? _____

2. Nouns belonging to the first declension are primarily which gender?
   _____

3. Why are the nouns **agricola** and **nauta** exceptions to the description above?
   _____

4. The nominative singular case endings **-us** and **-er (-r)** distinguish nouns of which
   declension? _____

5. What gender are the **-us** and **-er (-r)** nouns?_____

6. What is the third and final gender you must learn to identify?
   _____

7. What are five nouns of this gender?
   _____

8. Do any of these five nouns belong to the first declension? _____

9. How do you know? _____

10. To which declension do these five nouns belong? _____

11. What do they have in common with the masculine nouns that are also included in this

    declension? _____

12. Which neuter case endings are identical to those of the masculine words in the same
    declension? Indicate with an X.

	SINGULAR	PLURAL
NOMINATIVE	_____	_____
GENITIVE	_____	_____
DATIVE	_____	_____
ACCUSATIVE	_____	_____
ABLATIVE	_____	_____

13. Which case endings have you left unmarked?

    _____

B **The neuter rule; noun endings in -a** Note the following two-part rule.

- The accusative singular form of a neuter noun is always identical to its nominative singular form.

- The accusative plural form of a neuter noun is always identical to its nominative plural form.

The rule noted above, called the *neuter law,* holds true for neuter words in every declension.

The following nouns all end in **-a.** Because the words belong to different declensions, however, the endings provide different information about case and number.

Indicate the appropriate description of each term and then translate.

	FEM NOM SING	NEU NOM & ACC PL	TRANSLATION
1. frūmenta	_____	_____	_____
2. puella	_____	_____	_____
3. signa	_____	_____	_____
4. praemia	_____	_____	_____
5. littera	_____	_____	_____
6. via	_____	_____	_____
7. grātia	_____	_____	_____
8. cōnsilia	_____	_____	_____
9. pugna	_____	_____	_____
10. iniūria	_____	_____	_____

ROMANS AT HOME AND ABROAD

UNIT III REVIEW

A **Derivatives review** The list contains derivatives ending with the suffix *-al* or *-ial*, meaning *of, like,* or *relating to*. Complete each sentence with both the Latin source and the meaning of each word.

EXEMPLĪ GRĀTIĀ

Annual derives from **annus** and means *relating to* **the year**.

1. **Bilingual** derives from _____ and means *relating to* _____.

2. **Colonial** derives from _____ and means *relating to* _____.

3. **Essential** derives from _____ and means *relating to* _____.

4. **Filial** derives from _____ and means *relating to* _____.

5. **Formal** derives from _____ and means *relating to* _____.

6. **Habitual** derives from _____ and means *relating to* _____.

7. **Longitudinal** derives from _____ and means *relating to* _____.

8. **Magisterial** derives from _____ and means *relating to* _____.

9. **Material** derives from _____ and means *relating to* _____.

10. **Memorial** derives from _____ and means *relating to* _____.

11. **Occupational** derives from _____ and means *relating to* _____.

12. **Penal** derives from _____ and means *relating to* _____.

13. **Provincial** derives from _____ and means *relating to* _____.

14. **Signal** derives from _____ and means *relating to* _____.

15. **Social** derives from _____ and means *relating to* _____.

16. **Territorial** derives from _____ and means *relating to* _____.

17. **Visual** derives from _____ and means *relating to* _____.

18. **Vital** derives from _____ and means *relating to* _____.

19. **Vocational** derives from _____ and means *relating to* _____.

B Consider the italicized words in each of the following sentences. Circle the case needed to express the italicized words in Latin. Be sure to look at the context carefully before answering.

1. The owner of a recovered *runaway* sometimes marked that slave with an **F**.

   a. nominative **b.** genitive **c.** dative **d.** accusative **e.** ablative

   Do you know what the **F** stood for? _____

2. Many slaves, on the other hand, were loyal members of their households; to such slaves, a master could entrust highly specialized duties.

   a. nominative **b.** genitive **c.** dative **d.** accusative **e.** ablative

3. Slaves were *teachers, doctors, musicians,* etc.

   a. nominative **b.** genitive **c.** dative **d.** accusative **e.** ablative

   Can you name any other professions of slaves?

   _____

4. Appreciated slaves, moreover, might receive *gifts* of money.

   a. nominative **b.** genitive **c.** dative **d.** accusative **e.** ablative

   What could they do with this money?

   _____

5. Cicero's secretary, Tiro, was even freed by a special *decree*.

   a. nominative **b.** genitive **c.** dative **d.** accusative **e.** ablative

   Was there prejudice against freed men and freed women? Why or why not?

   _____

   _____

UNIT IV

ROMAN SOCIETY

LESSON XVII

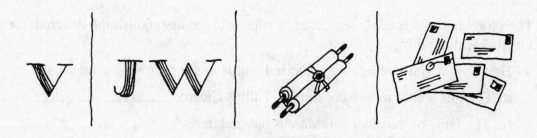

RŌMULUS ET NUMA ET TULLUS

 A **Vocabulary** Answer.

1. The noun **arma** in the vocabulary list for this lesson has no singular forms. What is its gender? _____

2. Which noun of the same gender (presented in Lesson XVI) also lacks the singular forms?

_____

3. Which sentence is correct?

    a. Arma est nova.   **b.** Arma sunt nova.

Notice that the ending **-a** on a neuter noun is plural. When it is used to indicate a subject, it requires a plural verb.

Compare the following.

    Concordia est grāta.   **Castra sunt in Galliā.**

Castra is not the only word you know with plural forms that are singular in meaning. Do you remember **littera?**

4. Using the words **littera** and **litterae,** label the drawings.

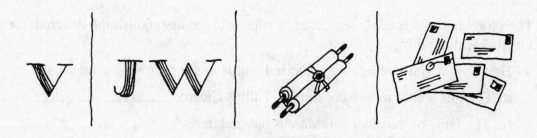

_____   _____   _____   _____

5. What three English letters were represented by the Roman letter in the first drawing?

_____   _____   _____

6. Translate the following sentence about the second drawing.

    Rōmānī litterās **J** et **W** nōn habuērunt.

_____

7. Translate the following into Latin.

There is a plan of war in the letter.

_____

8. Translate the following into Latin.

There is a large number of letters.

_____

The plural forms of some Latin nouns have special meanings. Use your glossary to find such a meaning for the new word **auxilium.**

auxilia = _____

Still other Latin nouns have meanings that are related, but not synonymous. **Nūntius,** for example, not only refers to a *messenger*, but also to the *message* that he or she carries. This new noun, **nūntius,** is interesting in yet another way. Compare the following.

servus, servī, (m.) *slave*

nūntius, nūntī, (m.) *messenger*

GENITIVE SINGULAR   NOMINATIVE PLURAL

Vīta serv*ī* dūra est.   **Serv*ī* nōn līberī sunt.**

Vīta nunt*ī* grāta est.   **Nūnti*ī* multās terrās vident.**

 The nominative plural nouns ending in **-ius** will always end in **-iī** (only the second **-ī** is the case ending). The genitve singular will end in one **-ī**. The base of such a noun, however, will still end in **-i:** *dative:* **filiō, nūntiō;** accusative: **filium, nūntium,** etc.

Therefore, in the preceding sentences, it is possible to distinguish the different forms of **nūntius** without difficulty.

9. How would you translate the italicized words in the following sentences?

    a. Quintus and Marcus were *sons* of Tullius Cicero. _____

    b. The fame of the older *son* Marcus has endured. _____

B **Irregular verb** *sum* One of the verbs that you have learned, although its principal parts are not regular, has the same personal endings as other verbs.

Translate.

1. sum _____

2. sumus _____

3. sunt _____

4. es _____

5. est _____

6. estis _____

In Lesson II, you learned two forms of yet another tense (**erat** and **erant**). This tense *(imperfect)* will be explained later. For now, recall that these two verb forms show a state of being that is past.

Translate.

7. erat _____

8. erant _____

Not all of these forms show the stem of the infinitive **esse (es-).**

Observe, however, that the perfect tense uses the stem **fu-** (from **fuī**) to form the perfect tense.

Translate two ways.

9. fuī _____   _____

10. fuimus _____   _____

11. fuistī _____   _____

12. fuistis _____   _____

13. fuit _____   _____

14. fuērunt _____   _____

C *Sum:* **present, future and perfect tense** Translate the following dialogue.

FĪLIUS: Fuistīne, Gaī, semper servus?

_____

SERVUS: Līber fuī in patriā meā. In terrā servus sum.

_____

SERVA: Fuimus magistrī in patriā nostrā. Nunc familiam tuam docēmus.

_____

SERVUS: Vīta servōrum nōn semper dūra est, sed virī vītam līberam semper amant.

_____

FĪLIA: Servam amō. Fuit magistra bona. Nunc est mea amīca bona.

_____

DOMINUS: Servī, labōrāvistus multum in familiā meā. Grātus sum quod servī bonī
            fuistis. Nunc servī nōn estis. Līberī estis.

_____

D *Sum:* **present, future and perfect tense** The future active tense forms of **sum** are introduced on page 127 of your textbook. As you can see, to conjugate **sum** in the future you use
the same vowel sequence (**ō, i, u**) that you already associate with the future tense of regular
verbs; the stem **er-** is the same as for the imperfect. Simply omit the **b.**

Refer to the list of verb forms on page 127.

15. What stem is common to all six forms of **sum** in the future tense? _____

Choose the correct answer.

16. Which of the following is future?
    a. est   **b.** fuit   **c.** erit   **d.** erat

17. Which of the following is not future?
    a. ero   **b.** estis   **c.** erimus   **d.** erunt

18. Which of the following is perfect?
    a. fuī   **b.** sumus   **c.** erant   **d.** eris

19. Which of the following is singular?
    a. erunt   **b.** estis   **c.** es   **d.** fuistis

20. Which of the following is not second person?
    a. eritis   **b.** fuistī   **c.** eris   **d.** sumus

LESSON XVIII

SPARTACUS

 Vocabulary As your knowledge of Latin vocabulary grows, many of the new words you encounter will resemble words that you already know. For each word, identify its part of speech and provide a definition.

EXEMPLĪ GRĀTIĀ

aequus	**aqua**	**equus**
(adj.) *just*	(noun) *water*	(noun) *horse*

1. altus   lātus

   _____   _____

2. amīcitia   amīcus

   _____   _____

3. castra   casa   causa

   _____   _____   _____

4. grātia   grātus

   _____   _____

5. habeō   habitō

   _____   _____

6. ibi   ubi

   _____   _____

7. mandō   maneō

   _____   _____

8. pugna   pugnō

   _____   _____

9. servō   servus

   _____   _____

10. via   vīta

    _____   _____

11. vērus   vester

    _____   _____

Name _____   Date _____

B **Questions in Latin** On pages 150–151 in your textbook, you can read about a famous catastrophe. The following Latin sentences tell a little more about it. To translate the questions in this exercise correctly, review pages 131–132.
You will need only the following words as supplemental vocabulary.

flamma, flammae (f.) *flame*
fūmus, fūmī (m.) *smoke*
lāva (this English word is actually
   an Italian noun, derived from a
   Latin verb. It is used in the
   sentences below as if it were a
   first declension noun.)
**dēvāstō, dēvāstāre, dēvāstāvī,
[dēvāstātus]** *destroy*

Translate.

1. Ubi est Vesuvius? Estne in Etrūriā? In Latiō?

_____

2. Nōnne in Campāniā est?

_____

3. Ubi erant Pompēiī*?

_____

* The name of the city **Pompēiī,** although it refers to a single place, is a plural noun.

4. Pompēiī erant oppidum ad Vesuvium.

_____

5. Annō Dominī LXXIX Vesuvius oppida Pompēiīs, Herculāneum et Stabiās* dēvāstāvit.

_____

_____

*Stabiae is another plural place name.

6. Nōnne Vesuvius populum terruit?

_____

7. Nōnne familiae fūmum et flammās vīdērunt?

_____

8. Nōnne ex oppidīs migrāvērunt? Num* in casīs mānsērunt?

_____

*Num: Questions introduced by this word expect the answer *No.*

9. Quis ad auxilium amīcōrum nāvigāvit?

_____

10. Ē lāva fōrmās multōrum virōrum līberāvimus.

_____

11. Estne Vesuvius nunc aequus?

_____

Name _____ Date _____

LESSON XIX

PATRŌNUS ET CLIENTĒS

 Third conjugation verbs Answer based on your reading.

1. You have learned to recognize verbs from two different conjugations. To determine whether a verb belongs to the first or second conjugation, which principal part do you look at?

   _____

Before proceeding, look closely on page 135 at the principal parts of the new verbs (*third conjugation*) that are presented in this lesson.

On the lines provided, supply the principal parts of each verb.

2. mātūrō _____ _____ _____

3. moveō _____ _____ _____

4. mittō _____ _____ _____

Among the preceding forms, **moveō** is obviously different. Like all second conjugation verbs, the first principal part of **moveō,** as well as its infinitive, tell you its conjugation. By contrast, based on their first principal parts alone, you cannot distinguish **mātūrō** from **mittō,** nor can you proceed to conjugate them correctly. You must learn how to find and use the present stems of these verbs.

One way to use the present stem is to create the imperative singular. You get the present stem (*singular imperative*) by dropping the **-re** of the second principal part.

EXEMPLĪ GRĀTIĀ

    Mātūrā! *Hasten!*   **Movē!** *Move!*

Following this pattern, supply and translate the singular imperatives of each third conjugation verb.

          IMPERATIVE   TRANSLATION

5. pōnō _____ _____

6. mittō _____ _____

7. cēdō _____ _____

For verbs of the first and second conjugations, the imperative plural is formed by adding **-te** to the present stem.

    Mātūrāte! *Hasten!*   **Movēte!** *Move!*

WORKBOOK
Copyright © by The McGraw-Hill Companies, Inc.

Give and translate the plural imperatives of each verb.

	IMPERATIVE	TRANSLATION
8. migrō	_____	_____
9. mereō	_____	_____

For third conjugation verbs, however, there is an important difference. The present stem vowel of these verbs (short **e**) remains in the imperative singular but becomes a short **i** in the imperative plural. Provide the plural imperatives and meanings according to the model supplied by **pōnō.**

		IMPERATIVE	TRANSLATION
pōnō	**pōne**	**pōnite**	**Put.**
10. **mittō**	**mitte**	_____	_____
11. **excēdō**	**excēde**	_____	_____

This vowel change from short **e** to **i** is an important characteristic of the third conjugation in the present tense. It is not limited to the imperative mood. Study the following examples.

Cēdite, captīvī.   **Cēdimus, domine.**

Translate.

12. _____

13. _____

As you can see, an **i** has replaced the stem vowel.

Excēditisne ex oppidō?   **Excēdō, sed amīcī meī nōn excēdunt.**

Translate.

14. _____

15. _____

Note in this last example that short **-i** changes to **-u** in the third person plural.

B **Verb stems** You must learn to recognize both the present and the perfect stems of a verb. Practice by circling all the stems in the verb forms below.

agere	ēgī
cēdere	cessī
accēdere	accessī
excēdere	excessī
dēfendere	dēfendī
mittere	mīsī
pōnere	posuī

C **Verb tenses: present, future, perfect** It is usually easy to identify the tense of a verb, because the two stems of a Latin verb are normally quite different, and the personal endings for present and perfect tenses are different.

Only in the third person singular present and perfect (ending **-it**) or the first person plural (ending in **-imus**) can the spelling of perfect and present be the same.

Indicate whether each verb is present, perfect, or both. Then translate each form.

	TENSE(S)	TRANSLATION
1. cēdunt	_____	_____
2. posuit	_____	_____
3. dēfendimus	_____	_____
4. mīsimus	_____	_____
5. accessistī	_____	_____
6. excessērunt	_____	_____
7. ēgistī	_____	_____
8. agunt	_____	_____
9. mittitis	_____	_____
10. dēfendit	_____	_____

D **Appositives** Read the following passage, then identify five appositives and the nouns they describe. Figure out the case and number of the appositive, then supply the Latin noun that correctly translates it.

Herculaneum, an Italian town, was buried by an eruption of the volcano Vesuvius. This town took its name from Hercules, a great hero.* To the inhabitants of the city, an affluent people, the hero's name gave particular pride. Among the ruins, archaeologists have found many statues of Hercules, signs of the public's devotion to its namesake.

*Vir can be translated *hero*.

APPOSITIVE	NOUN	CASE	NUMBER	LATIN
1. _____	_____	_____	_____	_____
2. _____	_____	_____	_____	_____
3. _____	_____	_____	_____	_____
4. _____	_____	_____	_____	_____
5. _____	_____	_____	_____	_____

LESSON XX

RŌMĀNĪ

 Present tense: third *-io* conjugation Answer.

1. Which stem vowel distinguishes the present active infinitives of the third conjugation?

_____

2. If the new verbs **capio** and **facio** (as well as their compounds) are classified in the same conjugation, what must the last three letters of their infinitives be?

_____

Another similarity can be seen in the imperative forms of these **-iō** verbs. Note:

cape	**pōne**
cap*ite*	**pōn*ite***

Notice, however, that the first and last forms of the present tense of these verbs are different from the others. Compare:

cap*iō*	pōnō	cap*imus*	pōn*imus*
cap*is*	pōnis	cap*itis*	pōn*itis*
cap*it*	pōnit	**cap*iunt***	pōnunt

Because of these two differences, verbs like **capiō, capere** are assigned to a different category called *third conjugation -iō*. They differ from third conjugation verbs in showing **-i** as part of their stem.

Answer the following questions.

3. What conjugation is **faciō**? _____

4. How do you know? _____

5. What conjugation is **nūntiō**? _____

6. How do you know? _____

7. Give the third person plural of **faciō** and **nūntiō** in the present tense.

_____   _____

 Fourth conjugation in present tense Obviously, not all verbs with first principal parts that end in **-iō** belong to the third conjugation. A large number of these verbs belong to the *fourth conjugation.* Your textbook presents third **-iō** verbs and *fourth conjugation* verbs together because they have much in common.

The most important difference is in the infinitives of this verb family. Because they are fourth conjugation verbs, infinitives of **mūniō, veniō,** and **inveniō** end in the letters **-īre,** not **-ere.**

A second difference is in the forms of the imperatives. The imperative forms of these new verbs *(fourth conjugation)* are formed according to the same rules as those of the first and second conjugations (stem or stem plus **-te**).

Since this is a familiar pattern, supply the missing forms below. Notice the long **-ī** in both the singular and plural forms of the fourth conjugation imperative, unlike third conjugation verbs like **capite, facite.**

CONJUGATION	INFINITIVE	SING. IMPERATIVE	PL. IMPERATIVE
1st	**vocāre**	_____	_____
2nd	_____	**valē**	_____
4th	_____		**venīte**

Principal parts and perfect stems Now that you have learned a number of third and fourth conjugation verbs, you can better appreciate the need to learn the principal parts. Notice how different most of the present and perfect stems of the following verbs are.

PRESENT	PERFECT
accēde-	**access-**
accipe-	**accēp-**
age-	**ēg-**
cape-	**cēp-**
cēde-	**cess-**
dēfende-	**dēfend-**
excēde	**excess-**
face-	**fēc-**
invenī-	**invēn-**
mitt-	**mīs-**
mūnī-	**mūnīv-**
pōne-	**posu-**
rege-	**rēx-**
venī-	**vēn-**

Translate.

1. invenit   invēnit

_____   _____

2. fēcimus   facimus

_____   _____

3. rēxistis   regitis

_____   _____

4. excēdunt   excessērunt

_____   _____

5. ēgistī   agis

_____   _____

D **Meanings of *agere*** Refer to the various meanings of **agere** found on page 144 in your textbook to translate the italicized words.

1. In a fit of madness sent by Juno, the hero Hercules murdered his family; afterwards, he *did much* to atone for this.

   _____

2. Once he had been ritually purified, he *pled* his *case* at Delphi.

   _____

3. He *talked* about *duties* with the Pythoness who spoke for the god Apollo at this oracle.

   _____

4. She taught him how he could pay for his deeds and attain immortality; thus, from that time—for twelve long years—he *spent* his *life* in servitude to King Eurystheus.

   _____

5. As one of ten labors assigned by this king, he *carried off loot* from the garden of Juno.

   _____

6. In Thrace, as yet another labor, he trapped and killed some man-eating mares; to do this, he first *drove the horses* into a flooded plain.

   _____

7. He often gave *thanks* to *Minerva and Vulcan* (**Volcānus, -ī**) who helped him greatly throughout his adventures.

   _____

LESSON XXI

AMĪCITIA

 A **Latin word order** If you have not done so already, study page 147 of your textbook. Remember that these observations about word order are not rules. However, they will help you to develop good translation habits.

Rearrange the words to create logical Latin sentences.

1. ā / accēpit / clārus / Eurystheō / Herculēs / multa / officia / vir

_____ _____ _____ _____ _____

Subject | Appositive | Nominative | Preposition | Ablative
(Proper noun | renaming | adjective | | object of
of the third | subject | modifying | | preposition
declension) | | appositive | |

_____ _____ _____

Accusative | Direct | Verb
adjective | object |
of quantity | |
preceding | |
its noun | |

2. ā / Graeciae / Hydrā / in / Lernā / populum / areā / servāvit

_____ _____ _____ _____ _____

Preposition | Ablative | Appositive | Genitive | Direct
of place | object of | renaming | following | object
where | preposition | object of | its noun |
| | preposition | |

_____ _____ _____

Preposition | Ablative | Verb
of place | object of |
from which | preposition |

 In sentence 3 below, **vaccās** (from **vacca, vaccae,** f., *cow*) is the direct object of both **invēnit** and **ēgit**. Latin is an economical language and will rarely repeat a word in such a sentence. **Taurum** (from **taurus, taurī,** m., *bull*) is similarly used in sentence 4 below.

Translate.

3. In īnsulā ad Hispāniam vaccās clārās invēnit et tum ad Graeciam ēgit.

_____

[Notice the two translations of **ad** that are used in this sentence.]

4. Auxiliō nautārum magnum taurum ē Crētā portāvit et Eurystheō dōnāvit.

_____

5. Eurystheus, nunc grātus, servum Herculem līberāvit.

_____

ROMAN SOCIETY

UNIT IV REVIEW

 A **Glimpses of Roman life: vocabulary review** Have you read pages 150–152? As you can see from that passage, a great variety of graffiti has survived from the days of ancient Rome: political slogans, advertisements, slander, and personal messages of every sort. The following English sentences present imaginary graffiti with something of that same range. To translate the italicized words in each, you must supply a Latin infinitive. The correct answers will spell a well-known motto about the timelessness of certain sayings.

1. Somebody ought *to free* us slaves.

2. Hey, aedile! Whose job is it *to fortify* these walls?

3. Flaccus hates *to hurry*.

4. If anyone deserves *to hold* office again, it's Statius. Vote for him.

5. Friends, Romans, countrymen, are you prepared *to do* your duty?

6. Watch out for you-know-who. They say he's itching *to rule*.

7. Who said we ought *to increase* our taxes?

8. Nobody wanted *to wait* for you, Afer. Sorry. We left.

9. My only choice is *to yield* to you, Cupid.

10. They really need *to put* new plumbing in these baths.

11. Dear Graeculus: Nobody ordered you *to come* here. Love it or leave it!

12. It's sweet *to take* naps in the afternoon.

13. Who are you trying *to scare* with the hairdo, Cressa?

14. Ruso knows how *to make* great pottery.

15. Wrap it up, Caesar. Nobody wants *to send* you more soldiers.

16. You're getting old, Villius. Ready *to depart?*

17. You may try *to defend* your honor, Marcellus, but most of us know the whole truth. Why bother?

18. Does anyone still remember Germanicus? That was a man who knew how *to lead* soldiers.

19. Everyone wants *to live* on the Palatine.

1. ___ |___| ___ ___ ___   ___ ___
2. ___ |___| ___ ___   ___ ___
3. ___ |___| ___ ___ ___   ___ ___ ___
4. ___ |___|
5. ___ |___|
6. ___ ___ ___ |___| ___ ___   ___ ___ ___ ___
7. ___ |___|
8. ___ ___ ___ |___| ___ ___ ___ ___   ___ ___ ___
9. ___ |___|
10. ___ ___ ___ |___| ___ ___   ___ ___ ___
11. ___ ___ |___| ___ ___   ___
12. ___ ___ |___| ___ ___ ___
13. ___ |___| ___ ___   ___ ___
14. ___ |___| ___
15. ___ |___| ___ ___ ___ ___ ___
16. ___ ___ ___ |___| ___   ___ ___ ___
17. ___ ___ ___ |___| ___ ___ ___   ___ ___ ___ ___
18. ___ ___ |___| ___   ___ ___ ___
19. ___ ___ ___ |___| ___   ___ ___ ___

Translate the Latin sentence that is spelled in the acrostic.

_____

B **Derivatives review** Each of the following nouns is the name of a profession or role and derives from a Latin word that you have learned. Use each noun once to answer questions 1 through 25.

advocate	curator	inspector	publisher
agronomist	debtor	inventor	reformer
amateur	doctor	liberator	victor
astronaut	donor	linguist	vocalist
clairvoyant	emigrant	navigator	
conductor	equestrian	novelist	
counselor	exterminator		

1. You have given blood to the Red Cross many times. You are a/an
   __ __ __ __ __.

2. You work for a company that makes books available to the public. You are a

   __ __ __ __ __ __ __ __.

3. You rid homes of bugs and rodents. You are an

   __ __ __ __ __ __ __ __ __ __ __.

4. You owe the government for your income tax. You are a __ __ __ __ __ __.

5. You study foreign languages. You are a __ __ __ __ __ __ __ __.

6. You run marathons for love and not for money. You are an

   __ __ __ __ __ __ __.

7. You take care of the artwork in a museum. You are a

   __ __ __ __ __ __ __.

8. You ran successfully for the position of city commissioner. You are an

   __ __ __ __ __ __ __ __.

9. You speak out for a movement that you have joined. You are an

   __ __ __ __ __ __ __.

10. You are moving overseas. You are an __ __ __ __ __ __ __ __.

11. You see the future clearly. You are a __ __ __ __ __ __ __ __ __ __ __.

12. You sail among the stars. You are an __ __ __ __ __ __ __ __ __.

13. You love to ride horses. You are an __ __ __ __ __ __ __ __ __ __.

14. You specialize in the management of farmland. You are an

    __ __ __ __ __ __ __ __ __ __.

15. You give advice. You are a __ __ __ __ __ __ __ __ __.

Name _____ Date _____

Select the word that describes the following individuals.

16. Simón Bolívar and Abraham Lincoln __ __ __ __ __ __ __ __

17. Benjamin Franklin and Thomas Edison __ __ __ __ __ __ __ __ __

18. Martin Luther and Martin Luther King, Jr. __ __ __ __ __ __ __ __ __

19. Leonard Bernstein and Seiji Ozawa __ __ __ __ __ __ __ __ __ __

20. Pearl S. Buck and Toni Morrison __ __ __ __ __ __ __ __

21. Jonas Salk and Christian Barnard __ __ __ __ __ __ __

22. Julius Caesar and Douglas MacArthur __ __ __ __ __ __

23. Madonna and Barbra Streisand __ __ __ __ __ __ __ __

24. Ferdinand Magellan and Christopher Columbus __ __ __ __ __ __ __ __ __ __

25. Sherlock Holmes and Inspector Clouseau (the Pink Panther) __ __ __ __ __ __ __ __ __ __

UNIT V

ROMAN POETS, GODS, AND HEROIC JOURNEYS

LESSON XXII

CERĒS ET PRŌSERPINA

A **Tense differences** The following Latin verbs (all second person singular present indicative) are distinguished by their stem vowels. Circle the stem vowel in each verb.

portās   docēs   pōnis   mūnīs

Valeō, valēre, because it belongs to the same group as **doceō** *(second conjugation),* will use its present stem vowel (long ē) to make the second person singular present indicative form.

Translate.

1. You are strong. _____

Regō, regere, however, because it is a third conjugation verb like **pōnō,** will change its present stem vowel (short **e**) to short **i.**

Translate.

2. You rule. _____

As a result, these two forms differ in spelling but express the same tense. They follow the rules for their conjugations.

Similarly, with the future tense, you must learn to recognize more than one tense sign. Verbs of the first and second conjugations follow one rule. However, another rule applies to the verbs of the third and fourth conjugations.

In the verbs **portābis** and **docēbis,** the letters **-bi-** tell you that these two forms express the future tense. The third conjugation is different, the tense signs are the vowels **a** and **e.**

Note that **a** as a sign of the future tense is limited to the first person singular. It is followed by the personal ending **-m** instead of **-ō.** (Think of **sum**).

3. **Pōnēs** means _____.

Translate.

4. You will be strong. _____

5. You will rule. _____

Carefully note the difference between the present and future tense forms of the third conjugation in the following sentence. Then translate the sentence into English.

   Nunc <u>regis</u>, sed nōn semper <u>regēs</u>.

6. _____

Note also the resemblance between present tense forms of the second conjugation and the future tense forms of the third conjugation in the following sentence. Then translate it into English.

Valēs et regēs.

7. _____

B **Recognizing future tense forms** It will not always be as hard to distinguish Latin verbs by tense as it was in the previous examples. More often, you will recognize the distinctive forms of stems and/or tense signs, as in the following examples. Determine the tense and conjugation of each verb form and then translate.

VERB	TENSE	CONJUGATION	TRANSLATION
1. dēbēbis			
2. excēditis			
3. migrābimus			
4. regam			
5. maneō			
6. dūcit			
7. dēfendunt			
8. exspectābunt			
9. mātūrāmus			
10. mittō			

The following verbs all have an **-e** before the personal ending, but differ in tense because they belong to different conjugations. Determine the tense and conjugation of each verb.

Nota•Bene To find whether the **-e** signals future or present tense, ask yourself: does the first principal part of the verb end in **-eō?** If it does, the **e** signals present tense because the verb is second conjugation. (e.g., **valēs <valeō** = you *are* well). If the first principal part ends in **-ō,** the verb having an **e** is future. (e.g. **regēs<regō** = you *will* rule).

VERB	CONJUGATION	TENSE	TRANSLATION
11. accēdes			
12. dēbēs			
13. habet			
14. aget			
15. dēfendēmus			
16. merēmus			

VERB	CONJUGATION	TENSE	TRANSLATION
17. tenētis	_____	_____	_____
18. dīcētis	_____	_____	_____
19. mittent	_____	_____	_____
20. terrent	_____	_____	_____

C **Practice** On pages 161–162 in your textbook, you read about the god of the Underworld, Pluto. The following passage supplies additional facts about Pluto, or Dis, as he was sometimes called by the Romans. Read the selection and then translate it.

Nota·Bene Note the following as you translate. Three regions of the Underworld are named **Erebus** (the location of Pluto's palace), *Tartarus,* and **Elysium.** The word **canis** *(dog)* in the third sentence is a third declension noun in apposition to **Cerberus,** the watchdog's name. Do you know what was unusual about Cerberus?

Plūtō dīcit:

Dominus populī magnī sum. In Erebō habitō et īnferōs regō. Clārus canis Cerberus terminōs terrae meae dēfendit. In agrīs Tartarī virōs malōs pōnō et in silvās Ēlysī virōs bonōs mittō. Poenās nūntiō et praemia dōnō.

Ad Siciliam, ubi pulchra Prōserpina habitat, equōs meōs agam. In carrō meō fīliam deae pōnam et tum excēdēmus. Num* probātis? Causam meam agam. Prōserpina amō. In Erebō rēgīna erit. Magnus deus sum. Nōnne grāta esse dēbet?

*Num introduces a question expecting *No* as an answer; *You don't... do you?*

_____
_____
_____
_____
_____
_____
_____
_____
_____
_____
_____

Name _____ Date _____

D **Third declension nouns** On pages 160–161, you will find a number of nouns that have unusual endings. These nouns belong to the third declension. You have already seen a number of them. The following names, for example, are both third declension nominative nouns.

Aristotelēs   Caesar

Plūtō, Herculēs and **Iūnō** are names that belong to the third declension. The nominative forms of third declension nouns, as you can see, can differ considerably. Despite this variation, the endings for all other cases are the same. It will prove useful for you to recognize them in your reading well in advance of learning the third declension endings in lesson XL.

Let's begin with the accusative singular ending. For both masculine and feminine forms, **-em** is used. Compare.

fōrm<u>am</u>   termin<u>um</u>   part<u>em</u> (line 19, page 161)

The ablative singular of a third declension noun is also fairly easy to recognize, especially when it identifies the object of a preposition or when it is modified by an adjective with a case ending that is clearly ablative. Compare.

hōr<u>ā</u>   ann<u>ō</u>   noct<u>e</u> (line 7, page 160)

Translate.

1. Ā Caesare fūgērunt.

_____

2. In planā parte agrī castra sunt.

_____

A third important ending is **-ēs,** the case ending for both nominative and accusative plural. Like **-em** and **-e,** it is used with both masculine and feminine words of the third declension.

EXEMPLĪ GRĀTIĀ

Multōs flōrēs vidēmus.

Flōrēs variī nōn sunt.   (lines 22–23, page 161)

Notice that in each of these examples you can tell the gender and case of the noun from its modifying adjective.

Translate.

3. Noctēs Iūnī et Iūlī* longae sunt.
  *Iūnius and Iūlius, of course, are the names of the months that the Romans used to call **Quinctilis** and **Sextilis.**

_____

4. In multīs pictūrīs, Cerēs sacrum flōrem* tenet.
  *Est papāver *(a poppy)*

_____

LESSON XXIII

LŪCIUS ET MĀRCUS

A **Adverbs** A very large number of the Latin adjectives that you know can form adverbs.

ADJECTIVE	MEANING	BASE	ADVERB	MEANING
pulcher, <u>pulchra</u>, pulchrum	*beautiful*	pulchr-	<u>pulchrē</u>	*beautifully*

Complete the following.

	ADJECTIVE	MEANING	BASE	ADVERB	MEANING
1.	_____	deep	_____	_____	_____
2.	_____	strange	_____	_____	_____
3.	_____	constant	_____	_____	_____
4.	_____	friendly*	_____	_____	_____
5.	_____	sacred	_____	_____	_____

*Note that the English word *friendly* is an adjective, even though it ends with the letters *-ly,* which often signify an adverb.

Instead of *friendlily,* which is correct but awkward, what English prepositional phrase would you be more likely to use? Hint: Start with *in . . . way.*

Bear in mind that not all adverbs are formed regularly. The adverb that corresponds to **bonus,** for example, is **bene.**

6. What does it mean? _____

Male, which means *badly,* is another unusual adverb. As you can see, it too ends with a short **e.**

As we have just seen, sometimes the adverbial forms of a familiar adjective will require a translation that does not end in *-ly.* **Plānē,** for example can either be translated *in a level manner* (to avoid the awkwardness of *levelly*) or *evenly* (since *even* is a good synonym of *level*). **Longē** is another good illustration of this, since it has to be translated *far.*

Translate.

Colōnī longē ā Rōmā migrāvērunt.

7. _____

Remember that not all Latin adverbs are formed from adjectives. You have already learned the following adverbs, which do not correspond to any adjective. Note that the meanings likewise do not end in -ly.

Translate.

8. ibi _____

9. nōn _____

10. nunc _____

11. semper _____

12. tum _____

13. ubi _____

B **Ablative of accompaniment** You now know two uses of the ablative case having the meaning *with:* the *ablative of means* and the *ablative of accompaniment.* It is usually easy to distinguish these two ablatives in Latin by looking at their usage.

Nota•Bene The *ablative of accompaniment* is used to express the idea of *company, companionship.* It is always written in Latin using the preposition **cum,** and it usually refers to people who are *together with* each other.

Rōmānī cum sociīs in concordiā habitāvērunt.
The Romans lived in harmony with their allies.

The *ablative of means,* by contrast, is used to express the idea of an *instrument* or *a tool used.* It *never* uses the Latin preposition **cum,** and it almost always involves *using a thing.*

Armīs patriam dēfendērunt.
With their weapons they defended the fatherland.

For each italicized phrase, consider its context and determine the type of ablative it would become in Latin.

    a. Means   (*with = by means of, using*)

    b. Accompaniment (*with = together with, along with*)

    c. Neither

1. _____   When Proserpina was small, she roamed the fields of Sicily *with Minerva and Diana.*

2. _____   *With violets* these goddesses once wove a bright blue mantle for their father Jupiter.

3. _____, _____   One day Pluto, *with his superior strength,* overcame Proserpina as she was playing in the fields. He rapidly transported her to Hades *with his chariot.*

4. _____   Heartsick *with grief,* the goddess Ceres searched the world for her missing daughter.

5. _____ At last, in a conversation *with Helios,* she learned of Proserpina's whereabouts.

6. _____, _____ *With great concern,* she then proceeded to Olympus where she plead *with Jupiter* for her daughter's freedom.

7. _____, _____ Finally, *with her powerful arguments,* Ceres prevailed. Proserpina thereafter was allowed to live *with her mother* for a portion of each year.

8. _____, _____ As soon as the harvest is over, however, *with great regret,* she returns each winter to reign *with her husband Pluto* in the kingdom of the dead.

C **Meanings of the preposition *in*** The preposition **in** can be used in more than one way. Its objects may be either ablative or accusative. When it is used with an ablative object, it means either *in* or *on,* and the construction is called *ablative of place where.*

in animō *in mind* **in terminō** *on the boundary*

When **in** is used with an accusative object, it means either *into* or even *onto.* When that object is a place the construction is called *accusative of place to which.*

in castra *into the camp*

A third use of the accusative with the preposition *in* is seen in this lesson. Note the change in meaning. **in Germānōs** *against the Germans*

Translate each sentence accurately with special attention to the italicized phrase.

1. Signa deōrum barbarōrum *in armīs sociōrum* erant.

_____

2. Menelāus Graecōs *in Troiam* incitāvit.

_____

3. Deī *in Olympō* habitant.

_____

4. *In Herculāneō* multae vīllae* pulchrae erant.

_____

* **vīlla, vīllae,** f. *country house*

5. Hannibal *in oppida** Italiae* bellum gessit.

_____

* **oppidum, -ī,** n. *town*

6. *In librīs Anglicōrum poetārum* multa verba pulchra dē glōriā Graeciae et Rōmae sunt.

_____

7. Nympha* ā deō *in silvam* fūgit.

_____

*nympha, -ae, f. fairy, nymph

8. *In annō* sunt I))MMMDCCLXVI* hōrae, minus XII minūtās.

_____

* The first three characters of this number, l)), are the Roman way of expressing 5000.

LESSON XXIV

PLĀGŌSUS ORBILIUS

 Vocabulary In the story of Orbilius, you learned the Latin suffix **-ōsus.** In English, the corresponding suffixes *-ose* and *-ous* are also signs of *fullness.*

EXEMPLĪ GRĀTIĀ

verbōsus	*verbose*	*using <u>too many</u> words*
glōriōsus	*glorious*	<u>*full of*</u> *glory*
iniūriōsus	*injurious*	*harm<u>ful</u>*

By analogy, can you supply the English derivatives and meanings of the following **-ōsus** words?

		DERIVATIVE	MEANING
1.	numerōsus	_____	_____
2.	grātiōsus	_____	_____
3.	bellicōsus	_____	_____
4.	officiōsus	_____	_____
5.	pretiōsus	_____	_____

Complete each sentence with either a partial or entire English word.

6. If a region is *populous,* it is full of _____.

7. A *captious* individual is fond of _____ing others in mistakes.

8. The *watery* fluid between the cornea and the lens of the eye is known as the _____ humor.

9. *Commodious* surroundings are full of _____.

10. If a source of information is *veracious,* it is _____ful.

B **Review of verb forms** In the last lesson, you learned two more verbs from the third **-iō** conjugation: **afficiō** and **incipiō.** You now know several verbs that belong to this group. Provide their meanings.

			MEANINGS
1.	capiō	capere	_____
2.	accipiō	accipere	_____
3.	incipiō	incipere	_____
4.	faciō	facere	_____
5.	afficiō	afficere	_____
6.	efficiō	efficere	_____
7.	fugiō	fugere	_____

Give all six forms of **incipiō** in both the present and perfect tenses. Include meanings.

	PRESENT (SING.)	MEANINGS
8.	_____	_____
9.	_____	_____
10.	_____	_____

	PRESENT (PL.)	MEANINGS
11.	_____	_____
12.	_____	_____
13.	_____	_____

	IMPERATIVE (S./PL.)	MEANINGS
14.	_____	_____

	PERFECT (SING.)	MEANINGS
15.	_____	_____
16.	_____	_____
17.	_____	_____

	PERFECT (PL.)	MEANINGS
18.	_____	_____
19.	_____	_____
20.	_____	_____

Fourth conjugation verbs, as you recall, have the same form as third conjugation **-iō**'s in the present tense, except that they frequently show long **-ī-**.

One of the most common fourth conjugation verbs, **audiō,** is introduced in this lesson. Give both the present and perfect tenses of **audiō.** Be sure to mark the macrons (long marks).

	PRESENT (SING.)	MEANINGS
21.	_____	_____
22.	_____	_____
23.	_____	_____

	PRESENT (PL.)	MEANINGS
24.	_____	_____
25.	_____	_____
26.	_____	_____

	IMPERATIVE (S./PL.)	MEANINGS
27.	_____	_____

	PERFECT (SING.)	MEANINGS
28.	_____	_____
29.	_____	_____
30.	_____	_____

	PERFECT (PL.)	MEANINGS
31.	_____	_____
32.	_____	_____
33.	_____	_____

Give the meaning of these fourth conjugation verbs.

MEANINGS

33.	audiō	audīre	_____
34.	mūniō	mūnīre	_____
35.	veniō	venīre	_____
36.	inveniō	invenīre	_____

C **Third -iō and fourth conjugation future tense** This lesson introduces you to the future tense of the third **-iō** and fourth conjugation verbs. These verbs use *the same tense signs and personal endings as third conjugation verbs.* Remember that **-i** or **-ī** always appears in the spelling of these verbs.

In the spaces provided below, give the future tense forms of **fugiō** *(third -io conjugation)* and **veniō** *(fourth conjugation).* Translate each form in the spaces provided.

	FUGIŌ	MEANINGS
1.	_____	_____
2.	_____	_____
3.	_____	_____
4.	_____	_____
5.	_____	_____
6.	_____	_____

	VENIŌ	TRANSLATIONS
7.	_____	_____
8.	_____	_____
9.	_____	_____
10.	_____	_____
11.	_____	_____
12.	_____	_____

D **Verb forms: present, future, perfect** Each set contains three forms of a verb in three different tenses. Translate each form.

1. accēpī _____

   accipiō _____

   accipiam _____

2. audīmus _____

   audiēmus _____

   audīvimus _____

3. effēcistī _____

   efficiēs _____

   efficis _____

4. invenient _____

   invenērunt _____

   inveniunt _____

5. fūgit _____

   fugit _____

   fugiet _____

E **Verb forms** Supply the missing verbs that correspond in person and number to the given form.

PRESENT	FUTURE	PERFECT
1. _____	_____	exspectāvit
2. continet	_____	_____
3. _____	_____	trāxit
4. _____	faciet	_____
5. audit	_____	_____

LESSON XXV

AENĒĀS

A **Vocabulary** Underline ten idioms and then translate each sentence.

1. Augustus cōnsilium magnum cēpit.

   _____

2. Multōs Rōmānōs convocāvit et verba fēcit.

   _____

3. Dē Rōmā ēgit. (Careful! This does not mean "he drove from Rome.")

   _____

4. "Nōn commodum est bella perpetua gerere."

   _____

5. "In terrīs variīs castra posuimus et multōs annōs cum barbarīs pugnāvimus. Armīs nostrīs grātiam* Rōmae auximus et glōriam meruimus. Terminōs novōs nunc habēmus at fāma nostra magna est. Sed augēre fōrmam* Rōmae nōn incēpimus. Templa nostra sunt parva et nostra loca pūblica nōn pulchra sunt."

   _____

   _____

   _____

   _____

   * what meaning is best here ?
   * *beauty* (literally, "shape")

6. "Nōnne deīs grātiam habētis? Populus grātus mūnīre multa templa dēbet."

   _____

7. "Nōnne cum familiīs vestrīs in ōtiō vītam agitis?"

   _____

8. "Multum ā Rōmā accēpistis et officium vestrum nunc est viās novās et monumenta* mūnīre."

   _____

   ***monumentum, monumentī,** n. *monument*

9. Augustus ā multīs Rōmānīs clārīs pecūniam accēpit et multum effēcit. Populus Rōmānus semper Augustō grātiās ēgit. "Rōmam laterīciam* invēnit; eam* marmoream* relīquit." *

_____

*laterīcius, -a, -um *brick*
*eam *it* (literally *her*, referring to Rome)
*marmoreus, -a, -um *marble*
*relinquō, relinquere, relīquī, [relīctus] *leave*

10. Vītam Augustī memoriā tenēmus et studium laudāmus.

_____

B **More about third declension nouns** Have you been noticing the third declension nouns in your readings? Sometimes, based upon the spelling of the nominative singular, you may think that such a noun actually belongs to the second declension. **Venus,** for example, looks like the proper noun **Mārcus,** but the genitive singular of her name is **Veneris,** not **Venī.** Because it ends in **-is,** it cannot be grouped with nouns of the second declension. It is a third declension noun.

Nota•Bene The genitive case ending is the sole factor that determines a noun's declension. All third declension nouns must have the genitive singular ending in **-is,** while all second declension nouns have a genitive singular ending **-ī.**

Translate.

1. socius Caesaris _____

2. fōrma flōris _____

This **-is** ending (*genitive singular*) must be distinguished from the **-īs** (*dat.* or *abl. pl.*) of the first and second declension.

Translate, observing the case endings.

3. Dē sententiīs Aristotelis agēmus.

_____

Let's briefly consider three other words that you have in Lessons XXIII and XXV: **māter** (*mother*), **pater** (**father**), and **frāter** (*brother*). These words, like **Venus,** look like second declension nouns at first. Their genitive singulars, however, are **mātris, patris,** and **frātris,** respectively, so they must be third.

Translate the following sentences.

4. Hecuba, rēgīna Trōiae, māter Creusae erat.

_____

(Creusa was the wife of Aeneas; she perished in the fall of Troy.)

5. Hector et Helenus erant frātrēs Creusae.

_____

(Hector also lost his life in the Trojan War; Helenus emigrated, however.)

6. Aenēās cum patre Anchīsā et fīliō Iūlō ē Trōiā excessit.

_____

(The nominative form of his father's name is **Anchīsēs.**)

The **-ēs** case ending, as you will recall, is usually either nominative, vocative, or accusative plural. Here are two examples from the story.

One is a proper noun, in the accusative case.

Aenēās Penātēs vīdit. (lines 16–17, page 173)

Another is a common noun, in the accusative case.

Nāvēs in aquam trāxērunt. (lines 12–13, page 173)

Translate accurately, observing the case endings.

7. Penātēs Aenēam docuērunt.

_____

_____

8. Nāvēs Troiānōrum ex Asiā nāvigāvērunt.

_____

_____

Note that **Aenēās** is not a third declension noun: the genitive singular form of this name is **Aenēae.** It is therefore a first declension masculine noun whose nominative case is irregular. Decline the phrase **Trōiānus Aenēās.**

	ADJECTIVE	NOUN
NOMINATIVE	_____	_____
GENITIVE	_____	_____
DATIVE	_____	_____
ACCUSATIVE	_____	_____
ABLATIVE	_____	_____

LESSON XXVI

POĒTA CLĀRUS

A **Vocabulary** Use **-que** to complete each sentence.

1. _____ *(to the Greeks and the Romans)*
   grātiam habēmus.

2. Ex _____ *(Athens and Rome)* multum
   accēpimus.

   [All forms of **Athēnae** are plural; **Rōma,** of course, is a singular noun.]

3. Multī _____ *(boys and girls)* nunc memoriae
   linguam Latīnam mandat.

4. Dē Rōmānīs _____ *(they read and write).*

5. Ē librīs sententiās _____ *(many and varied)*
   dē Rōmā trahunt.

B **Imperfect tense active** Note that the imperfect tense has several possible translations.

EXEMPLĪ GRĀTIĀ

legēbam   I *was* gathering
I *used to* gather
I *kept on* gathering
I gathered
I *would* (ordinarily, usually) gather

Referring to the model above, translate the following verbs in five different ways.

labōrābāmus   **scrībēbant**

1. _____   6. _____

2. _____   7. _____

3. _____   8. _____

4. _____   9. _____

5. _____   10. _____

Notice that one of the acceptable translations for the imperfect tense is the same as a translation of the perfect tense.

	IMPERFECT	PERFECT
I gathered	**legēbam**	**lēgī**

The difference, obscured in this last translation, is that the *imperfect* expresses *action occurring over a period of time,* while the *perfect* emphasizes *completed* action.

Translate into Latin.

		IMPERFECT	PERFECT
11.	you *(sing.)* began	_____	_____
12.	she held	_____	_____
13.	we heard	_____	_____
14.	you *(pl.)* sent	_____	_____
15.	they watched	_____	_____

Perfect vs. imperfect tense In many instances, however, it will be clear that only one of these tenses can be accurately used. Determine the appropriate tense for each sentence and write "perfect" or "imperfect."

1. You have sent money. _____

2. You used to send money. _____

3. He was holding the standard. _____

4. He has held the standard. _____

5. We have not heard the report. _____

6. We kept on hearing the report. _____

7. We were beginning to yield. _____

8. We did begin to yield. _____

9. They would not watch the fight. _____

10. They did not watch the fight. _____

LESSON XXVII

AD ITALIAM

 A **Vocabulary** One of the words in this lesson is an adjective with a plural form only.

paucī, paucae, pauca

EXEMPLĪ GRĀTIĀ

Paucī captīvī erant.

Translate.

1. _____

It resembles another adjective that you learned earlier.

singulī, singulae, singula

Singulī captīvī fūgērunt.

Translate.

2. _____

Like **medius, -a, -um** *middle (of),* and **reliquus, -a, -um** *rest (of),* which you learned earlier, the adjective **paucī** does not require genitive case nouns to follow it. *Few* and *few (of)* are both acceptable meanings for this word.

 B **Active and passive voice** The difference between the active and the passive voice is important. Consider the following.

I kiss. **Basiō.**   *I am (being) kissed.* **Basior.**

 If the subject *performs* the action, the voice of the verb is active. If the *action* of the verb affects the subject, it is in the passive voice. In the above example, the present passive voice in English is formed with the present tense *am* plus a *past* tense form.

Do not let this confuse you. Determine whether each phrase is active or passive by considering simply whether the subject is *acting* or *being acted* upon. This is a completely different question from the tense (time) the action is occuring.

Name _____ Date _____

Tell whether the following verbs are active or passive voice.

VOICE

1. we are holding _____

2. we have held _____

3. we are not held _____

4. we did hold _____

5. you used to lead _____

6. you do lead _____

7. were you being led? _____

8. you will be led _____

9. he is being freed _____

10. he has freed _____

11. he will be freed _____

12. he is freeing _____

13. they do not listen _____

14. will they be heard? _____

15. they kept on watching _____

16. they used to be ruled _____

17. I am being afflicted _____

18. am I leading? _____

19. I shall make _____

20. I have been afflicted _____

Compare the active and passive personal endings for the present, imperfect, and future tenses:

	ACTIVE	PASSIVE	MEANING
S.	ō/m	r	I
	s	ris	you
	t	tur	(he/she/it)
PL.	mus	mur	we
	tis	minī	you (all)
	nt	ntur	(they)

Name _____ Date _____

C **Passive voice** Identify the tense, person, and number of each of the following passive verbs.

	PERSON	NUMBER	TENSE
1. docēbar	_____	_____	_____
2. docēbitur	_____	_____	_____
3. docēminī	_____	_____	_____
4. docēris	_____	_____	_____
5. docēbimur	_____	_____	_____
6. capiuntur	_____	_____	_____
7. capientur	_____	_____	_____
8. capiēbatur	_____	_____	_____
9. capior	_____	_____	_____
10. capiēbāminī	_____	_____	_____

Now translate the preceding *passive* verb forms in the spaces provided. Once you have done that, give the corresponding *active* forms and translate them into English.

	PASSIVE TRANSLATION	ACTIVE FORM	ACTIVE TRANSLATION
1.	_____	_____	_____
2.	_____	_____	_____
3.	_____	_____	_____
4.	_____	_____	_____
5.	_____	_____	_____
6.	_____	_____	_____
7.	_____	_____	_____
8.	_____	_____	_____
9.	_____	_____	_____
10.	_____	_____	_____

Name _____ Date _____

 D **Passive voice: English to Latin translation** Translate only the italicized words in each sentence. Be sure to use the correct person, number, tense and voice. Note also that the form of the verb depends on its conjugation (1st, 2nd, 3rd, etc.)

1. The winds *are being ruled* by Aeolus.

   _____

2. Their care *is entrusted* to him by Jupiter.

   _____

3. They are all *held together* in a cave.

   _____

4. From time to time, at the god's command, a single wind *will be driven* from its prison.

   _____

5. At other times, many *will be set free* to toss the waves.

   _____

LESSON XXVIII

AENEĀS IN ĀFRICĀ

 Vocabulary One of your new vocabulary words, **appellāre,** is unusual. It means *to call,* but it differs from **vocō** in usage. **Appellāre** means t*o call by name,* or simply *to name,* **vocāre** means **call to** or *summon.*

In the active voice, **appellāre** often takes two accusatives: *to call somebody something.*
Translate.

1. Barbaram terram Graeciam appellāvērunt, quod Graecī eam *(it)* tenuērunt.

_____

The second of these two accusatives, **Graeciam,** is often called a *predicate accusative* to indicate that it is a noun being identified with the direct object (here, **terram**). Do not worry about the terminology. Just be aware that verbs like **appellāre** *(name),* and **facere** *(make)* may take two accusative nouns, one of which is identified with the other.

In the passive voice, **appellāre** often requires a *predicate nominative:*

Translate.

2. Aeolus appellātur dominus ventōrum.

_____

Notice that **dominus** is nominative. The passive forms of **appellō,** therefore, are used like linking verbs.

A similar pattern is often observed with the passive forms of **video.** The best translation of this verb is the English word *seem* rather than the passive voice *am, is,* or *are seen.* The predicate nominative construction is again used.

Translate.

3. Nōn grātī vidēminī.

_____

4. Cōnsilium bonum vidētur.

_____

In these last examples, the adjectives **grātī** and **bonum** are both predicate nominatives.

B **Transitive and intransitive verbs** Give the principal parts and meanings of each intransitive verb. Note that all intransitive verbs in this text are signaled by a fourth principal part ending in **-ūrus.**

PRINCIPAL PARTS   MEANINGS

1. _____   *-āre*   _____   migrātūrus   _____
2. _____   _____   _____   properātūrus   _____
3. _____   _____   _____   mānsūrus   _____
4. _____   _____   _____   valitūrus   _____
5. _____   _____   _____   cessūrus   _____
6. _____   _____   _____   accessūrus   _____
7. _____   _____   _____   excessūrus   _____
8. _____   _____   _____   fugitūrus   _____
9. _____   _____   _____   ventūrus   _____
10. _____   _____   _____   conventūrus   _____

C **Transitive and intransitive verbs** Identify each active verb below as transitive or intransitive, then translate.

Nota•Bene   Remember that an active intransitive verb does not transfer its action to a direct object. Intransitive verbs also cannot be put into the passive voice; e.g. "remain" makes no sense in the expression "I am remained" (passive), only "I am remaining" (active).

TRANSITIVE / INTRANSITIVE   TRANSLATION

1. mānsistis   _____   _____
2. capit   _____   _____
3. properāvimus   _____   _____
4. convocābat   _____   _____
5. veniam   _____   _____
6. dēfendis   _____   _____
7. excēdent   _____   _____
8. inveniunt   _____   _____
9. tenet   _____   _____
10. sumus   _____   _____

 **D** **Active to passive voice** Since the subject of a passive verb receives action instead of initiating it, there can be no such thing as the direct object of a passive verb.

Study the following.

S.   D.O.
Rōmānī barbar*um* ex Italiā agu*nt*.

The Romans drive the foreigner out of Italy.

AGENT   S.
Ā Rōmānīs barbarus ex Italiā agi*tur*.

By the Romans the foreigner is being driven out of Italy.

 Nota•Bene The preceding sentences convey the same information in two very different ways. In the first sentence, **Rōmānī** is the subject of an active verb and **barbarum** is the direct object. In the second sentence, **barbarum** becomes the subject **barbarus,** while **Rōmānī** becomes an ablative of agent **ā Rōmānīs,** "by the Romans." Then the verb **agunt** is made passive (**agitur**) and agrees with its new subject, **barbarus,** in having a third person singular ending **–tur.** Everything else in the second sentence stays the same.

Compare the second example above with the following.

ABL.MEANS SUB.
Armīs Rōmānīs barbar*us* ex Italiā agitur.

The foreigners are driven out of Italy by means of/with Roman arms.

The ablative of means here expresses *what things are used* to accomplish a given end. In the sentence beginning with **Armīs,** observe that the arms are the means by which the foreigner is expelled.

In the second example, **ā Rōmānīs** *(the Romans)* are the agents, or actors, by whom the foreigners are driven out. The ablative of agent expresses *not how,* but rather by whom an action is accomplished. It uses a preposition (**ā, ab),** and identifies the person or people responsible for the action.

 **E** **Differences in ablatives** Since you have learned to translate the preposition **ā, ab** as *from* or

Nota•Bene Simply remember that the preposition can be *by* only if it appears in a clause with a passive verb. However, when the verb is active, **ā, ab** will most likely mean *from,* even if its object is a person.

away from, this new meaning to express agency may seem difficult.
Translate:

1. Aenēās ā deīs auxilium accēpit.

_____

When, on the other hand, the object of **ā, ab** is a place or thing, it will always mean *from,* no matter what voice the verb is.

2. Aenēās ab officiō trahitur. (Remember: ab officiō is not ablative of means!)

_____

Learn to distinguish between these two uses of the preposition, the ablative of agent, and the ablative of separation/place from which.

3. Aenēās ab officiō ā pulchrā rēgīnā trahitur.

_____

Types of ablative:

- *ablative of separation*   **ab officiō**
- *ablative of personal agent*   **ā pulchra rēgīnā**

Translate with particular attention to the italicized phrases.

4. *Ā Poeniciā* * rēgīna Dīdō *cum multīs sociīs* nāvigāvit.

_____

*Phoenicia

5. *Ā virō malō** fugiēbat.

_____

**her brother Pygmalion*

6. *Ā Sychaeō** et cōpia pecūniae et via ad Āfricam rēgīnae monstrābantur.

_____

_____

**Sychaeus, her murdered husband*

7. *Pecūniā* Dīdō *ā barbarīs* terram parāvit.

_____

8. Tum *ā Poenīs** oppidum magnum, Carthāgō, *in novā* terrā muniēbātur.

_____

**the Phoenicians (Carthaginians)*

9. Ad Carthāginem* Aenēās Trōiānīque reliquī *ventīs undīsque* afficiuntur. *Auxiliō Neptūnī* servantur.

_____

Remember that **ad can sometimes mean near.*

10. *Ā rēgīnā* Trōiānī in templō pulchrō accipiuntur.

_____

11. *Ā templō* ad magnam cēnam ducuntur.

_____

12. Aenēās verba facit et *ā multīs* spectātur et laudātur.

_____

13. Sed *ā deā Venere* Dīdō movētur; *verbīs Aenēae* tenētur et incitātur.

_____

ROMAN POETS, GODS, AND HEROIC JOURNEYS

UNIT V REVIEW

A **Derivatives: compound verbs** Now that you know a number of verbs such as **capiō** that are used as the bases of compounds (e.g. **accipiō, incipiō**), you perhaps appreciate Latin prepositions more than ever. The following activity uses prefixes based upon four prepositions—**ad, in, e(x),** and **cum**—as well as the prefix **re-**. Use your English dictionary when necessary.

Define each prefix in as many ways as possible.

1. ad _____

2. in _____

3. e(x) _____

4. cum _____

5. re _____

Let's begin with five derivatives of **cēdō.** Note that your answers use both the present stem and the participial stem *(fourth principal part).* Note also that the spelling of the prefixes (especially **ad** and **cum**) may change their last letter to match the first letter of the word to which it is joined (e.g. **ad + firmus** becomes *affirm*). We call this phenomenon *assimilation* (see pages 107, 111, and 168 of your text).

cēdo, cēdere, cessī, [cessūrus]

ad + cēdō

6. If you are looking for an *approach* to your destination, you are in search of an _____ *(n.).*

in + cēdō

7. When a noise *does not yield,* we call it _____ *(adj.).*

ex + cēdō

8. What do you do when you *go beyond* your quota in the Latin Club candy sale? You _____ *(v.)* it!

cum + cēdō

9. If you *give in* on a particular point while arguing with someone, you are said to _____ *(v.)* to that person.

re + cēdō

10. Sometimes after a nation's economy has been moving forward rapidly and steadily, it *moves backwards.* This setback is called a _____ *(n.).*

vocō, vocāre, vocāvī, [vocātus]

ad + vocō

11. If a woman *voices* her support to move an organization *toward* a position of prominence, she is an _____ (n.) of its causes.

in + vocō

12. A public ceremony is often opened by a speaker who *calls upon* a god or a saint to bless the program. Such an appeal is called an _____ (n.).

ex + vocō

13. A sensory stimulus, such as a melody or the scent of a flower, can *call out* a memory. The word _____ (adj.) describes such stimuli.

cum + vocō

14. The presiding officer of a group is about to *call* its members *together* for a meeting. He will _____ (v.) them.

re + vocō

15. If the terms of a contract do not allow it to be *called back* for cancellation, it is an _____ (adj.) agreement.

valeō, valāre, valuī, [valitūrus]

ad + valeō

16. You plan to take advantage of a situation in order to *strengthen* your personal position. You will _____ (v.) yourself of this opportunity.

in + valeō

17. Your teacher has listened to your explanation of why an important assignment is late. She does *not* regard your case as a *strong* one, however; in her opinion, you have offered an _____ (adj.) excuse.

ex + valeō

18. If you have been hired to work out an assessment of a new program's *strengths* and weaknesses, your job is that of an _____ (n.).

cum + valeō

19. A very sick individual has gradually become *altogether well;* his period of recovery can be referred to as a time of _____ (n.).

re + valeō

20. An expert has appraised your rare stamp collection at a price far below what you think it is worth. You plan to ask another authority to _____ (v.), or make a *new estimate* of its worth again.

dūcō, dūcere, dūxī, [ductus]

ad + dūcō

21. Do you know the name of the muscle that *leads* your thumb *toward* your forefinger when you make the signal "OK" with your hand? It is call an _____ *(n.)*.

in + dūcō

22. You have been *drawn into* military service. You are an _____ *(n.)*.

ex + dūcō

23. If you are able to *draw* a conclusion *out of* your study of certain data you can _____ *(v.)* its significance.

cum + dūcō

24. Her many wild escapades acting *together* have not *led* her to a state of inner tranquility; adventures of that nature are not _____ *(adj.)* to composure.

re + dūcō

25. In arithmetic, you sometimes have to *draw* a fraction *back* to its lowest equivalent terms. When you do this to the fraction, you _____ *(v.)* it.

capiō, capere, cēpī, [captus]

ad + capiō

26. You are not satisfied with your friend's comments, and you do not *take* them *to* heart. In your opinion, they do not constitute an _____ *(adj.)* apology.

in + capiō

27. He could feel the familiar symptoms just *beginning* to come *upon* him; he had an _____ *(adj.)* head-cold.

ex + capiō

28. The coach treats one of your teammates differently. By *taking* this student *out* of certain mandatory activities, he makes an _____ *(n.)* out of him.

cum + capiō

29. You often come up with original ideas that reflect your *complete grasp* of abstract notions *together*. Because you can deal with such generalized terms, you are know as a good _____ *(adj.)* thinker.

re + capiō

30. If you have a boss who readily *takes* your ideas *back* for consideration, you work for a _____ *(adj.)* individual.

veniō, venīre, vēnī, [ventūrus]

ad + veniō

31. Do you enjoy *coming* to the end of a familiar road and driving on into the unknown? If so, you love _____ *(n.)*.

in + veniō

32. Under the pressure of difficult circumstances, many people *come upon* new ways of handling old problems. In other words, their hardships force them to become _____ *(adj.)*.

ex + veniō

33. If a positive *outcome* is clearly foreseen, we wait for final, or _____ *(adj.)* success.

cum + veniō

34. Each summer the members of the Junior Classical League _____ *(v.)*, or *come together,* for competition, instruction, and fellowship.

re + veniō

35. Money that *comes back* to the government from taxes and the sale of licenses is called _____ *(n.)*.

UNIT VI
MISSION TO A NEW WORLD: AENEAS AND ROME

LESSON XXIX

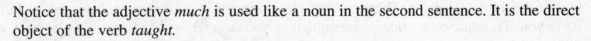

AENĒĀS ET DĪDŌ

 A **Words used as nouns** Any word used as a noun is called a *substantive*. A pronoun, for example, is a substantive because it is a part of speech that can replace a noun. Compare the following sentences.

> *The Muses once taught <u>Apollo</u>.*

> *They once taught <u>him</u>.*

Notice that in the second sentence, both the subject and the direct object of the first sentence have been replaced with pronouns. Pronouns are just one type of substantive.

Adjectives can also be used substantively.

> *They taught him the arts of the lyre and poetry.*

> *They taught him <u>much</u> about music.*

Notice that the adjective *much* is used like a noun in the second sentence. It is the direct object of the verb *taught*.

Another kind of substantive is a verbal, such as an infinitive.

> <u>*To create*</u> *is <u>to be inspired</u> by Apollo and the Muses.*

Notice that the two infinitives in the preceding sentence are also used like nouns. *To create* is the subject of the sentence, and *to be inspired* functions as a predicate nominative.

Finally, consider the following sentence.

> *Ancient poets hoped <u>that the Muses would direct their work</u>.*

What did they hope? Notice that in this sentence an entire clause (*that the Muses would direct their work*) functions as the direct object of the verb *hoped*.

 Three of the adjectives that you have learned are often used substantively. Define them as adjectives and then as nouns.

	MEANING AS ADJECTIVE	MEANING AS NOUN
1. amīca	_____	_____
2. barbarus	_____	_____
3. finītimus	_____	_____

Information about gender and number is always expressed in the ending of a Latin adjective. This information is particularly important when translating substantives.

Malus accēdit.   *A bad man is approaching.*

Bonae fugiunt.   *The good women are fleeing.*

Match the following Latin substantives to their correct English translations.

4. _____ bona   **a.** a good man

5. _____ nostrī   **b.** the truth (a true thing)

6. _____ mea   **c.** many people

7. _____ bonus   **d.** many things

8. _____ misera   **e.** our men

9. _____ malum   **f.** goods

10. _____ multī   **g.** misfortune (a bad thing)

11. _____ vērum   **h.** bad people

12. _____ malī   **i.** poor woman

13. _____ multa   **j.** my things

B **Revisiting the third declension** In a previous workbook lesson, you studied some case endings of the third declension. These endings have recurred in your readings and may be familiar to you. Translate each sentence to strengthen your awareness of context clues to help with third declension case endings.

1. Ā populō Rōmānō <u>nāvēs</u> Pompēiō* dōnābuntur.

_____

Gnaeus Pompēius Magnus, a.k.a. Pompey the Great

Besides being plural, how does **dōnābuntur** help to identify **nāvēs** as a subject?

_____

2. Ā Rōmānīs <u>noctēs</u> in quattuor vigiliās* dīvidēbantur.

_____

* **vigilia, vigiliae,** f. *(night) watch*

What case ending appears on the subject of this sentence?

_____

3. <u>Flōrēs</u> pulchrōs in Siciliā vidēbitis.

_____

In the preceding sentence, is the word **flōrēs** nominative or accusative? How do you know?

_____

4. Sextus appellor; quīnque <u>frātrēs</u> habeō.

_____

 In this sentence, **quīnque** does not have an ending that indicates the case of **frātrēs.** How can you tell whether **frātrēs** is the subject or the direct object of the verb?

_____

LESSON XXX

AENEĀS AD ĪNFERŌS

 Vocabulary The reading selection in this lesson introduces a number of new words. You can learn some valuable derivatives from each of these words. Complete the activity below using the dictionary in your textbook and an English dictionary.

LATIN WORD	ITS MEANING	ENGLISH DERIVATIVE	ITS MEANING
1. aurum	_____	aurous	_____
2. īnferus	_____	inferior	_____
3. lacrima	_____	lachrymose	_____
4. rāmus	_____	ramified	_____
5. somnus	_____	somnolent	_____

B **Past perfect and future perfect tenses** In this lesson, your textbook introduces two additional tenses of the Latin verb: the *past perfect (pluperfect)* and the *future perfect*. Since there are only six tenses in the Latin language, you have reached an important stage in your study of grammatical forms.

The English translation of the *pluperfect* tense uses the helping verb *had* to express action finished *before* another past action. To understand this tense better, it helps to review both the imperfect and the perfect tenses. Compare the underlined words in the following sentences.

As you proceed through the first few units of your textbook, <u>you kept on memorizing</u> (imperfect) *set after set of endings.*

At this point, therefore, <u>you have memorized</u> (perfect) many forms.

As soon as <u>you had memorized</u> (past perfect) them, you could recognize them quickly and translate them easily.

Using the second person singular and the idiom **memoriae mandāre,** translate the underlined expressions from the preceding sentences into Latin.

1. _____

2. _____

3. _____

The English translation of the future perfect tense uses two helping verbs, *will have* (or, where appropriate, *shall have).* Compare the underlined words in the following sentences.

So far, <u>you have learned</u> (perfect) four tenses of Latin verbs. In this lesson, <u>you will learn</u> (future) *two more tenses. By the end of the lesson, <u>you will have learned</u> (future perfect) the active forms of all six tenses of Latin verbs.*

Using the second person singular and the verb **nōscere,** translate the underlined phrases from the preceding sentences.

4. _____

5. _____

6. _____

Nota•Bene   Because the verb **nōscere** means *to learn,* its perfect tense can be translated in two ways: *to have learned* or *to know.* Once you *have* learned something, you know it. Compare and study the following translations of specific forms of **nōscō.**

nōvī	*I know* *(I have learned)*
nōveram	*I knew* *(I had learned)*
nōverō	*I will know* *(I will have learned)*

Verb tenses: imperfect vs. past perfect; future vs. future perfect   Complete the following chart using appropriate stems and personal endings. Start by identifying the person and number of the form provided in each set, and then create corresponding forms in the other two specified tenses.

IMPERFECT	PERFECT	PAST PERFECT
1. _____	appellāvistī	_____
2. retinēbat	_____	_____
3. _____	_____	āmīserāmus
4. _____	incēpistis	_____
5. conveniēbant	_____	_____

FUTURE	PERFECT	FUTURE PERFECT
6. _____	_____	convocāveritis
7. _____	auxērunt	_____
8. procēdam	_____	_____
9. _____	affēcit	_____
10. audiēmus	_____	_____

D **Future perfect vs. future** The following sentences are based on Greek and Roman myths. As you translate the italicized words in each set, pay careful attention to the tense and voice of the verbs. Be sure to use the appropriate Latin stems.

1. LEANDER TO HERO:

I will look (= will have looked) for a signal before I swim across to you.

_____

HERO TO LEANDER:

I will have placed a torch in the tower to guide you through the darkness.

_____

2. PYRAMUS TO THISBE:

Because we love each other, *we will flee* from Babylon.

_____

By this time tomorrow, *we will have begun* a new life in another place.

_____

3. Soon, on the island of Naxos, the cries of the abandoned Ariadne *will be heard* and she will be comforted.

_____

Bacchus *will have come* to her rescue.

_____

4. JUNO TO ECHO:

Wretched nymph! Because you have deceived me, *I will take* from you all but your voice.

_____

Then *you will know (will have learned)* the strength of my anger.

_____

5. On the morning after the wedding, forty-nine of Danaus' daughters *will show* their father their husbands' corpses.

_____

One *will not have done* her duty.

_____

E **Verb synopsis** Now that you have learned all these forms, you can give thirty-six active variations of each Latin verb that you know (every person and number for each of the six tenses). However, you can demonstrate your knowledge without going into such detail. A convenient way of doing this is by giving one verb in all tenses, but for only one specified person and number. This is called a *synopsis*.

EXEMPLĪ GRĀTIĀ

regit	*she rules; she is ruling; she does rule*
regēbat	*she was ruling; she used to rule*
reget	*she will rule; she will be ruling*
rēxit	*she ruled; she has ruled; she did rule*
rēxerat	*she had ruled*
rēxerit	*she will have ruled*

The order of the arrangement is fairly logical: the first three tenses all come from the present stem, while the second three are all based on the perfect stem. The first three tenses involve *continuing action,* while the second three involve *completed action.*

you are watching	Going on at this time (present)
you were watching	Going on before this time (imperfect)
you will be watching	Going on after this time (future)
you have watched	Completed prior to the present time (perfect)
you had watched	Completed prior to a past time (pluperfect)
you will have watched	Completed prior to a future time (future perfect)

Create your own Latin/English synopsis in the third person plural using the English verb *to eat dinner* (**cēnō, cenāre, cēnāvī, cēnātus**).

VERB FORM   MEANINGS

1. _____   _____
2. _____   _____
3. _____   _____
4. _____   _____
5. _____   _____
6. _____   _____

F **Substantives** Did you notice the following substantives in the reading selection on page 211? How did you translate them?

1. multa nova   *(line 8)*   _____
2. vērum   *(line 10)*   _____
3. malī, malōs   *(lines 14, 18)*   _____
4. bonōrum   *(line 15)*   _____

LESSON XXXI

AENĒĀS IN ITALIĀ

 Derivatives In the course of your Latin studies so far, you have become familiar with the names of many Roman deities. These names are often the sources of interesting derivatives. See how many of the following you can identify.

1. One of the verbs in this lesson (**cupiō**) is related to the name of a Roman deity. This god was often referred to as *Amor*. Name him.

   _____

   _____

2. **Cupiō** also gives us an English word that means *greed*. Identify that word.

   _____

3. The mother of *Amor* was special to the Romans. From her name, they derived a word that means *to worship*. Give both her name and its derivative.

   _____

4. The names of our third and sixth months also derive from the names of Roman gods. Which months and gods are these?

   _____ ; _____

   _____ ; _____

5. The mother of Proserpina, about whom you read in Unit V, was the goddess of the harvest. Name her and the food group which is named for her.

   _____ ; _____

6. Yet another deity, who presided over the forge, was said to live on the island of Sicily. The fires of Mt. Aetna were believed to be signs of his activity. As a result, all mountains which emit smoke and flames have been named for this god. Who was he, and what are such mountains called?

   _____ ; _____

7. The ruler of the Underworld lived far from his fellow deities on Mt. Olympus. We refer to the outermost planet of our solar system by his name.

_____

8. One of the gods was particularly noted for his rapidity of movement. From his name we have taken a word that describes a swiftly changeable temperament. Give both the name and its derivative.

_____ ; _____

9. In classical art, the ruler of the gods was often portrayed with an expression which has been called *jovial.* By what more common name do we know this god?

_____

What is the meaning of *jovial?*

_____

10. A number of sentences in the workbook have referred to the adventures of the hero Hercules. What is meant by the expression, *a Herculean task?*

_____

B **Personal pronouns** Pronouns sometimes help to make a subject more specific. Translate the following pairs of sentences. Remember that when a subject is expressed in the nominative case, you will not translate the personal ending of the verb.

1. Rōmam laudāmus.

_____

Ego et familia mea Rōmam laudāmus.

_____

2. In patriā remanēbitis.

_____

Tū et amīcus tuus in patriā vestrā remanēbitis.

_____

3. Ad īnsulam nāvigāverant.

_____

Is et ea ad īnsulam nāvigāverant.

_____

4. Spectābat.

_____

Is spectābat. *(or)* Ea spectābat.

_____

The vocative forms of personal pronouns are the same as their nominative forms. Translate each sentence.

5. Tū, excēde nōbīscum.

_____

6. Ubi fuistis, vōs puerī malī?

_____

Since some forms of the personal pronouns (like **nōs** and **vōs**) can be used to express more than one case ending, it is important to check for subject–verb agreement.

Translate each sentence.

7. Inimīcī nōs vīdērunt.

_____

8. Nōs inimīcī sumus.

_____

9. Nōs inimīcōs nostrōs vīdimus.

_____

10. Vōsne terruī?

_____

11. Vōsne ā mē terrēbāminī?

_____

12. Māter mē et amīcum meum ad tē, pater, mīsit.

_____

13. Nōnne pecūnia ā tē et familiā tuā dēbēbātur?

_____

14. Litterāsne prō nōbīs scrībēs?

_____

15. Nōbīs, nōn vōbīs, praemium dōnābit.

_____

16. Aut vōbīscum aut sine vōbīs prōcēdēmus.

_____

Name _____ Date _____

C **Personal pronouns and pronominal possessive adjectives** Once when the people of Rome were hiding in their citadel, a maiden named Tarpeia was approached by the enemy.

Translate the italicized pronouns in the following dialogue, paying close attention to the case, gender, and number required. If the word is an adjective, make it agree in case, number, and gender with the word it describes.

1. SABINES: *We* have come from the hills east of Rome.

   _____

2. TARPEIA: Although you are *my* enemies, I will show *you* the way.

   _____   _____

   But *you* must promise to give *me* a reward.

   _____   _____

3. SABINES: What shall we give *you?*

   _____

4. TARPEIA: I want the bronze on *your* arms.*

   _____

   *bracchium, bracchī, n. *arm*

5. SABINES: Very well, but first you must lead *us* to the citadel.

   _____

6. TARPEIA: I will guide *you* along a secret path. Follow *me* closely.

   _____   _____

   Now *I* have brought you with *me* to the citadel itself.

   _____   _____

   Where is *my* reward?

   _____

7. SABINES: We shall honor *our* word.

   _____

   Along with the bronze, however, *you* shall also receive a punishment that suits a traitor.

   _____

Tarpeia's request for "bronze" had not been specific enough, and as a result she received something she was not expecting. Do you know what her fate was? (Hint: What else, besides bracelets, would soldiers have been carrying on their arms?)

   _____

D Verb tenses Translate.

1. aberat _____

2. āfuerat _____

3. dubitāvistī _____

4. dubitāveras _____

5. cupiunt _____

6. cupīverant _____

7. dīmittimus _____

8. dīmīsimus _____

9. fuerint _____

10. fuērunt _____

LESSON XXXII

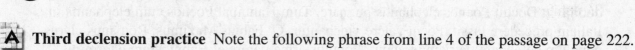

Q. FABIUS MAXIMUS

A **Third declension practice** Note the following phrase from line 4 of the passage on page 222.

perpetuō labōre

1. Footnote 4 tells you that **labōre** is ablative. How do you know, based on the phrase itself, that the noun labor is not feminine?

_____

2. **Arcem** (line 5) is also a third declension noun. What is its case?

_____

You have now encountered the following case endings which are shared by masculine and feminine nouns of the third declension.

**THIRD DECLENSION
MASCULINE / FEMININE**

	SINGULAR	PLURAL
NOMINATIVE	(any)	-ēs
GENITIVE	-is	
DATIVE		
ACCUSATIVE	-em	-ēs
ABLATIVE	-e	

Translate into Latin using the third declension endings for the words above:

3. She took on a great labor.

_____

4. They fought in front of the citadel.

_____

Name _____ Date _____

B **Subject and object infinitives** Review and study the uses of the infinitive that are given on pages 128 and 223 of your textbook. Then translate the following passage.

Hannibal, Poenus clārus, bellum gerere in Rōmānōs properāvit. Poenī, inimīcī Rōmānīs, cupīvērunt Rōmam in prōvinciam redigere. In Hispaniā Hannibal proelium committere nōn dubitāvit. Docuit Poenōs elephantīs pugnāre. Tum Hannibal Poenōs cum elephantīs in Italiam prōcēdere iussit. Poenī valēre vidēbantur. Q. Fabius Maximus, Rōmānus clārus, populum dēfendere patriam incitāvit. Populus arma parāre et Hannibalem ē terminīs agere mātūrāvit.

_____

_____

_____

_____

_____

_____

_____

_____

1. Which sentences from the passage do not contain an infinitive with an accusative subject? Write the accusative subjects and infinitives and give the line number.

_____

LESSON XXXIII

AENĒĀS ET TURNUS

 Perfect passive participle Answer based on your reading.

1. The fourth principal part of a verb can be used like what other part of speech? (Think of how many endings it has.)

   _____

2. What is the grammatical name for such a verb form?

   _____

3. What is the fourth principal part of the Latin verb **prōpōnō?**

   _____

4. What is the fourth principal part of the Latin verb **suscipiō?**

   _____

5. What tense and voice are the two principal parts that you have given above?

   _____   _____

Supply the correct form of each italicized participle. Be careful to supply the correct case, number, and gender based on what word the participle is describing.

6. The opinion *proposed* by the tribune will not be approved.

   _____

7. We accepted the opinions *proposed* by the people.

   _____

8. The plan *undertaken* by the settlers was excellent.

   _____

9. Did you approve the plans *undertaken* by the settlers?

   _____

 Perfect passive tense The subject of the first sentence (*a proposed opinion*) is grammatically similar to the sentence *An opinion was proposed*. To express either thought in Latin, a participle is necessary.

However, in the second sentence, a form of **sum** must be used as a helping verb for the participle, creating a two-part verb. This two-part construction agrees with its subject in two ways: the first part agrees in case and number, the second (a form of **sum**) agrees in person and number. *An opinion was proposed* is **sententia prōposita est.**

When forms of **sum** are used in this way, they are no longer translated as they are when used alone. Notice that **est** in this phrase does *not* mean "is." This variation in meaning of the forms of **sum** in combination with the perfect passive participles is one of the chief difficulties of the perfect passive tenses.

Translate and compare the verb forms used in the following sentences.

1. PATER: Fīlium meum fīliamque meam properāre iubeō.

   _____

   Līberōs meōs properāre iussī.

   _____

2. FĪLIUS: Properāre iubeor.

   _____

   Properāre iussus sum.

   _____

3. FĪLIA: Ego etiam properāre iubeor.

   _____

   Ego etiam properāre iussa sum.

   _____

4. LĪBERĪ: Properāre iubēmur.

   _____

   Ā patre nostrō properāre iussī sumus.

   _____

C **Perfect, past perfect, and future perfect passive tenses** Identify the tense and voice of each of the following Latin verbs.

	TENSE	VOICE
1. sum	_____	_____
2. appellāta sum	_____	_____
3. eram	_____	_____
4. ductus eram	_____	_____
5. erō	_____	_____
6. audītus erō	_____	_____

7. In all six tenses, what voice is the independent use of **sum**?

   _____

8. What voice is expressed by the use of **sum** with a participle?

   _____

D **Passive voice** Match each of the following Latin verbs with its English translation.

1. _____ missa est   **a.** he will be sent
2. _____ missa erunt   **b.** it will have been sent
3. _____ missum est   **c.** they had been sent
4. _____ mittētur   **d.** she has been sent
5. _____ missae sunt   **e.** they were being sent
6. _____ mittēbantur   **f.** they will have been sent
7. _____ missus est   **g.** they are sent
8. _____ mittuntur   **h.** they have been sent
9. _____ missī erant   **i.** it was sent
10. _____ missum erit   **j.** he has been sent

E **Passive voice** Translate each sentence.

1. Multōs annōs nautae Rōmānī ā pīrātīs terrēbantur.

_____

2. Etiam Iūlius Caesar ā pīrātīs captus erat.

_____

3. Removēre pīrātās erat magnum officium, et quod vir ēgregius erat officium Pompēiō mandātum est.

_____

4. Tum in Asiā cum aliīs* inimīcīs bellum ā Pompēiō gestum est.

_____

*other

5. Propter* victōriās Pompēius appellātus est "Magnus."

_____

*on account of

LESSON XXXIV

NIOBĒ

 Vocabulary Many Latin words resemble one another in spelling. As your vocabulary increases, therefore, you must learn to distinguish among these look-alikes. Keep the following facts in mind.

Often the vowel quantities of identically spelled forms will differ.

    līber (long **i**)   *free*   **liber** (short **i**)   *book*

Since the words that look alike are often different parts of speech, their use in context will frequently assist you.

Tantalus nōn līber erat, sed in Tartarō tenēbātur.
Tantalus was not free, but he was held in Tartarus.

Clārus liber poētae Vergilī multa dē Tartarō nārrat.*
The famous book of the poet Virgil tells many things about Tartarus.
*****Nārrō** means to *relate.*

(The famous book, of course, is the *Aeneid*.)

Note the difference in the stem between these two words:

   ADJECTIVE STEM   **līber**

   NOUN STEM   **libr**

Multī librī in Alexandriā erant.
Many books were in Alexandria.

Magistrī puerōrum Rōmānōrum nōn līberī sed servī erant.
The teachers of Roman boys were not free men but slaves.

Gracchī, Tiberius Gāiusque, erant līberī Cornēliae, Rōmānae clārae.
The Gracchi, Tiberius, and Gaius, were the children of Cornelia, a famous Roman woman.

Translate the entire sentence, paying special attention to underlined words.

1. Linguam barbaram <u>novī</u>.

_____

2. Nōvistīne terminōs verbī <u>nōvī</u>?

_____

3. Mēdicus* sum et vītam <u>servō</u>.

_____

*****medicus, -ī, m.** medic, doctor

4. Mēdicō, <u>servō</u> ēgregiō, vītam tuam mandā.

_____

5. Nōnne servōs tuōs <u>līberās</u>?

_____

6. Ad terrās <u>līberās</u> prōcēdent.

_____

7. <u>Pugnā</u> oppidum recipiēs.

_____

8. <u>Pugnā</u>, Rōmāne!

_____

9. <u>Portās</u> nostrās relīquistī*, socī, sed nōn ex animīs nostrīs excessistī.

_____

  *relinquō, relinquere, relīqui, relictus: leave back, leave

10. Tēcum amīcitiam nostram <u>portās</u>.

_____

B **Present passive infinitives** The infinitives that you know are present active infinitives; this lesson introduces you to the present passive infinitives for all four conjugations. Review your textbook reading before attempting this exercise.

Translate the following infinitives into Latin.

 1. to call _____

 2. to see _____

 3. to lead _____

 4. to receive _____

 5. to find _____

Translate into English.

 6. vocārī _____

 7. vidērī _____

 8. dūcī _____

 9. accipī _____

 10. invenīrī _____

Complete the chart.

PRESENT ACTIVE INFINITIVE	TRANSLATION	PRESENT PASSIVE INFINITIVE	TRANSLATION
11. convocāre	_____	_____	_____
12. līberāre	_____	_____	_____
13. merēre	_____	_____	_____
14. iubēre	_____	_____	_____
15. scrībere	_____	_____	_____
16. trahere	_____	_____	_____
17. afficere	_____	_____	_____
18. cupere	_____	_____	_____
19. audīre	_____	_____	_____

Try the procedure with a verb that you have not yet learned.

| 20. impedīre | _____ | _____ | _____ |

 Present passive infinitive form Be careful not to confuse the present passive infinitive with other verb forms ending in **-ī**. Circle the present passive infinitive in each group of words, carefully distinguishing it from perfect active verb forms and perfect passive participles.

1. gerī   gessī   gestī

2. scrīpsī   scrībī   scrīptī

3. trīctī   trahī   trīxī

4. cupīvī   cupītī   cupī

5. dīmissī   dīmīsī   dīmittī

In the next five groups of words, circle the *perfect passive participle*.

 Remember that this form has all the endings of any first and second declension adjective. However, for the purposes of this exercise, only forms ending in **-ī** have been used.

6. prōposuī   prōpositī   prōpōnī

7. nōtī   nōscī   nōvī

8. suscipī   suscēpī   susceptī

9. interfēcī   interfectī   interficī

10. reductī   redigī   redēgī

D **Present passive infinitive in English** Translate the italicized words in each sentence and then answer the questions.

1. I do not want *to be loved* by Apollo. I would rather be a tree. Who am I?

   _____

   _____

2. I want my fortune *to be increased* by the golden torch. Who am I?

   _____

3. I want my forty-foot gold and ivory statue *to be placed* in the most beautiful building in the world. Who am I?

   _____

4. As Rome's thirteenth emperor, I want a massive campaign in Dacia *to be undertaken* immediately by my soldiers. Who am I?

   _____

5. As Rome's fourteenth emperor, I want our British holdings *to be fortified* from sea to sea by a great wall. Who am I?

   _____

MISSION TO A NEW WORLD: AENEAS AND ROME

UNIT VI REVIEW

 A **Characters in the *Aeneid*** Using this list, identify the characters described below. Write their names in the designated spaces. If your answers are correct, the aligned letters will spell out a sentence vertically.

AENEAS	ANNA	IULUS	LAVINIA	SIBYL
AEOLUS	DIDO	JUNO	MERCURY	TURNUS
AMOR	FATES	JUPITER	NEPTUNE	VENUS
ANCHISES	HELENUS	LATINUS	PENATES	VULCAN

1. This man is the hero of Vergil's epic poem.

2. Angry at the interference of Juno, he calms a storm that has threatened the Trojan fleet.

3. He is sent to recall Aeneas to his mission.

4. This goddess is full of anger toward the Trojans.

5. An Italian prophetess, she guides Aeneas through the Underworld.

6. This Carthaginian princess encourages her sister to welcome Aeneas.

7. He dies in Sicily, but is briefly reunited with his son in the Elysian fields.

8. For love of Aeneas, this dedicated queen neglects her kingdom.

9. The Julian clan claimed him as their ancestor.

10. This hostile prince opposed the settlement of Trojans in Italy.

11. She was an Italian princess whom Aeneas was destined to marry.

12. Another survivor of the war at Troy, this prophetically gifted king advises Aeneas en route to Italy.

13. Aeneas and a Rutulian noble were rivals for the hand of this king's daughter.

14. One of the minor deities, he accepts a bribe from Juno to hurt the Trojans.

15. This god, a brother of Aeneas, impersonates Aeneas' son.

16. From the workshop of this God, Aeneas' mother obtains special armor.

17. During the fall of Troy, she finds Aeneas and tells him to flee.

18. Aeneas and his men bear these gods from their fatherland to a new home across the sea.

19. Despite his wife's opposition, this god directs Aeneas to his journey's end.

Answers

1. ___
2. ___
3. ___
4. ___
5. ___
6. ___
7. ___
8. ___
9. ___
10. ___
11. ___
12. ___
13. ___
14. ___
15. ___
16. ___
17. ___
18. ___
19. ___
20. ___

Sentence: _____

_____

Translation: _____

_____

UNIT VII
SCHOOLS, SITES, AND SIGHTS IN THE ROMAN EMPIRE

LESSON XXXV

LŪDĪ RŌMĀNĪ ET NOSTRĪ

A **Vocabulary** The preposition introduced in this lesson closely resembles a preposition that you already know. Be sure to distinguish carefully, between **ā, ab** *(away from, by)* and **ob** *(on account of, for)*. **Ab** governs the ablative case; **ob** governs the accusative. Both are used as prefixes in English and Latin.

Define these derivatives of **teneō,** based on the Latin root and prefixes **ab** and **ob.**

1. abstain _____

2. obtain _____

B **Vocabulary** Recall that **lūdus** means *game, play, show,* or *school.* Since all of these involved (at least from the Roman point of view) an element of make-believe competition or simulated action, many English derivatives of the verbal stem **lūd-, lūs-** contain these ideas.

The following list contains words that derive from the verb **lūdō.** Complete each sentence by choosing a word from the list.

allusion   illusion
allusive   illusory
collusion   interlude
deluded   ludicrous
elusive   prelude

1. Roman comedies may have begun with a _____ *(preliminary skit)* to get the audience seated and paying attention before the actual play started.

2. Stage sets for comedies typically depicted three adjacent house façades creating the _____ *(mock appearance)* of a city street.

3. In comic plots, slaves and ambitious young people were shown pursuing _____ *(deceptively hard to attain)* goals such as freedom, love, and wealth.

4. _____ *(deceived or made fun of)* masters and fathers were often the laughing-stocks of these plays.

5. The comic endings enjoyed by the ancients are _____ *(full of play)* because they involve such improbable and hard to believe outcomes.

The following list contains words that derive from **dō.** Complete each sentence by choosing a word from the list.

additional	pardon
condone	perdition
data	render
date	surrender
edition	traditional

6. It is a fateful _____ *(given point in time)* for King Agamemnon. He has just returned from a ten-year absence at Troy and does not realize that his wife Clytemnestra is plotting to kill him.

7. She cannot find it in her heart to _____ *(forgive)* Agamemnon for the death of her daughter Iphigenia. Since he went away, therefore, she has assumed complete power and has taken a new husband named Aegisthus.

8. These two will not _____ *(give up)* authority to the returning hero.

9. The resulting murder of the king condemns his household to _____ *(a state of being given over to ruin).*

10. The outcome of this dramatic cycle portrays the _____ origin of Athenian justice *(a version repeatedly given in oral accounts).*

Nota•Bene Now that you have learned the verb **dō,** you will rarely encounter **dōnō,** except in its special sense of donating, or making a presentation.

C **First conjugation parts and stems** Give the specified stems for the following verbs.

PRESENT STEM

1. habitō _____

2. mandō _____

3. probō _____

PERFECT STEM

4. amō _____

5. mōnstrō _____

6. nāvigō _____

PARTICIPIAL STEM

7. nūntiō _____

8. occupō _____

9. parō _____

STEM

10. pugnō *(imperfect active)* _____
11. spectō *(imperfect passive)* _____
12. dubitō *(future active)* _____
13. convocō *(pluperfect passive)* _____
14. servō *(future perfect active)* _____
15. appellō *(perfect passive)* _____
16. dōnō *(present active)* _____
17. incitō *(future passive)* _____
18. dō *(perfect active)* _____
19. labōrō *(pluperfect active)* _____
20. laudō *(present passive)* _____

LESSON XXXVI

TEMPLA DEŌRUM

 Independent and subordinate clauses As you know from your studies of English grammar, a *clause* is a group of words containing a *subject* and a *verb*. It expresses an action about a subject, but it is not necessarily a complete, self-contained thought. Units of thought containing subject and verb that depend on others to complete their meaning are called *subordinate clauses*.

Indicate which of these word sequences are independent clauses based on the criteria above. Do not consider capitalization or punctuation.

1. _____ because he cannot be here

2. _____ why can't he be here

3. _____ who cannot be here

4. _____ of whom we spoke

5. _____ we spoke of him

Indicate which of the following are subordinate clauses based on the criteria above.

6. _____ for which it stands

7. _____ to whose advantage

8. _____ of thee I sing

9. _____ what so proudly we hailed

10. _____ with a grain of salt

 Subordinating ideas using relative clauses *Relative clauses* are one kind of subordinate (dependent) clause. In each of the sets below, create one sentence by *subordinating* the information in the second sentence. The italicized words in the first sentences should be your antecedents. Note that there are several correct ways to combine these sentences.

EXEMPLĪ GRĀTIĀ

Gemellus has recently married *Maronilla*.
Maronilla is an unattractive and elderly woman.

Gemellus has recently married *Maronilla, who* is an unattractive old woman.

 The names and the humorous anecdotes that you will use in this activity derive from the collected epigrams of the Roman poet Martial.

Name _____ Date _____

Following the preceding model, combine each set of sentences.

1. *Diaulus* has become an undertaker.

   Until recently, Diaulus was a doctor.

   _____

2. Laecania has white *teeth;* Thais' *teeth* are black.

   Laecania's teeth are dentures; Thais' teeth are her own.

   _____

C **Relative clauses, pronouns, and antecedents** Identify the relative clauses in the following sentences by placing them within brackets [ ]. Next, underline the subject once and the verb twice in each clause. Then, circle the relative pronoun and draw an arrow to its antecedent.

EXEMPLĪ GRĀTIĀ

History has preserved the fame of Alexander, [who was born to King Philip of Macedonia and Queen Olympias of Epirus].

1. Alexander was taught by a famous Greek philosopher, whose name was Aristotle.

2. The young prince received a wild horse to whom he gave the name Bucephalus, meaning *ox-head;* on this animal, he later rode to many victories.

3. After he subdued the kingdom of Persia, he met Roxane, a beautiful princess, whom he married.

4. At last, in India, he recognized a truth about which he wept: there were no more worlds to conquer.

D **Sentences with relative clauses in Latin** In order to analyze and successfully translate complex sentences, you must learn to identify key elements in a sentence. In each sentence, circle the relative pronoun, draw an arrow to its antecedent, and then bracket the relative clause. Finally, fill in the blanks.

1. Ōlim in Forō Rōmānō erat magnum fissum* quod Rōmānōs terrēbat.

   gender of antecedent   _____

   number of antecedent   _____

   case of relative pronoun   _____

   case use of relative pronoun _____
   *fissum, -ī, n. *crack, fissure*

2. Ab ōrāculō* cuius sententia petīta erat populus causam fissī nōverat.

   gender of antecedent   _____

   number of antecedent   _____

   case of relative pronoun   _____

   case use of relative pronoun _____
   *ōrāculum, -ī, n. *oracle, prophecy*

3. Ōrāculum dīxerat: "Legite thēsaurum* ēgregium ē cōpiā bonōrum quae habētis et pōnite thēsaurum in fissum."

gender of antecedent _____

number of antecedent _____

case of relative pronoun _____

case use of relative pronoun _____

*thēsaurus, -i, m. *treasure, savings*

4. "Tum fissum quod vōs terret removēbitur et glōria Rōmae aucta erit."

gender of antecedent _____

number of antecedent _____

case of relative pronoun _____

case use of relative pronoun _____

5. Virī doctī dē ēgregiō thēsaurō ēgērunt et populō nūntiāvērunt: "Animus noster quī ā fīnitimīs nostrīs vīsus est et laudātus est, ēgregius thēsaurus Rōmānōrum est."

gender of antecedent _____

number of antecedent _____

case of relative pronoun _____

case use of relative pronoun _____

6. Inter Rōmānōs quī verba ōrāculī audīvērunt erat Mārcus Curtius, vir clārus.

gender of antecedent _____

number of antecedent _____

case of relative pronoun _____

case use of relative pronoun _____

7. Ad Forum properāvit in equō quōcum in fissum ruit.*

gender of antecedent _____

number of antecedent _____

case of relative pronoun _____

case use of relative pronoun _____

*ruit *he rushed*

8. Per annōs in memoriā populī Mārcus Curtius tentus est ob exemplum quod prōposuit.

gender of antecedent _____

number of antecedent _____

case of relative pronoun _____

case use of relative pronoun _____

LESSON XXXVII

COLOSSĒUM

 A **Vocabulary: compound verbs** What do you notice about all four of the verbs in the vocabulary list for this lesson? For each word, list the prefix and a simpler form of the verb, along with the meanings of both.

PREFIX	BASIC VERB	PREFIX MEANING	VERB MEANING
1. _____	_____	_____	_____
2. _____	_____	_____	_____
3. _____	_____	_____	_____
4. _____	_____	_____	_____

Determine which Latin verb is the best translation for the italicized word in each sentence.

      a. āmittere   **e.** mittere
      b. committere   **f.** permittere
      c. dīmittere   **g.** submittere
      d. intermittere

5. _____ All Roman tribes *sent* voting representatives to the Comitia.

6. _____ Citizens of every social class *entrusted* their concerns to respected spokesmen.

7. _____ These individuals *lost* no opportunity to speak on behalf of their constituents.

8. _____ Romans *allowed* every citizen a chance to state his views.

9. _____ They never *interrupted* a filibuster.

10. _____ Moreover, they never *dismissed* an issue without discussion.

11. _____ The practices of this democratic assembly *furnished* our founding fathers with the model for the House of Representatives in the United States.

Review the meanings of the following verbs. Then determine which verb is the most appropriate translation for the italicized word in each sentence. (Hint: consider a Latin word's English derivatives for help.)

      a. continēre   **d.** sustinēre
      b. obtinēre   **e.** tenēre
      c. retinēre

12. _____ A Roman rarely *held* forks or knives.

13. _____ Their **triclinium,** or dining room, *held* three couches.

14. _____ A rigid seating etiquette *held* at banquets.

15. _____ Although the table was repeatedly cleared during the course of a meal, the guest often *held back* a portion of his food as leftovers to be taken home.

16. _____ A wealthy Roman gave dinners frequently and *held* many clients by his patronage.

Name _____ Date _____

B **Second conjugation principal parts and stems** Review the principal parts of the second conjugation verbs. Remember that the verbs of the first conjugation form their principal parts according to a regular pattern. However, the second conjugation does not follow a regular pattern. Indicate the appropriate designation for each stem with an X.

	PRESENT	PERFECT	PARTICIPIAL
1. habit-	_____	_____	_____
2. habu-	_____	_____	_____
3. iubē-	_____	_____	_____
4. iuss-	_____	_____	_____
5. vīd-	_____	_____	_____
6. vidē-	_____	_____	_____
7. vīs-	_____	_____	_____
8. auct-	_____	_____	_____
9. aux-	_____	_____	_____
10. augē-	_____	_____	_____

Using your knowledge of second conjugation stems, identify the person, number, tense, and voice of each verb. Then translate each.

	PERSON	NUMBER	TENSE	VOICE	TRANSLATION
11. manēmus	_____	_____	_____	_____	_____
12. mānsimus	_____	_____	_____	_____	_____
13. valuērunt	_____	_____	_____	_____	_____
14. valuerint	_____	_____	_____	_____	_____
15. mōvistis	_____	_____	_____	_____	_____
16. mōtī estis	_____	_____	_____	_____	_____
17. movēbātis	_____	_____	_____	_____	_____
18. sustenta est	_____	_____	_____	_____	_____
19. sustinuit	_____	_____	_____	_____	_____
20. sustinet	_____	_____	_____	_____	_____

C **Ablative of manner** The distinction between *means* and *manner* is the difference between a *tool* and a *behavior*. While both ablative of means and ablative of manner answer the question "how?", the ablative of manner indicates the *behavior or manner of acting* that describes how the action is done. In Latin, the *ablative of means* never uses a preposition. The *ablative of manner* may or may not use a preposition.

carrō	*with a cart, by means of a cart*
cum cūrā	*with care, carefully*

In phrases expressing manner, whenever nouns are modified by an adjective, the preposition **cum** may appear between its object and the modifier, as follows:

EXEMPLĪ GRĀTIĀ

cum magnā cūrā

= *with great care; very carefully*

magnā cum cūrā

The Romans, in fact, seemed to prefer this word order.

It is even possible to express such a phrase without a preposition.

magnā cūrā   *with great care; very carefully*

However, remember that the preposition can be omitted only if an adjective is used.

For each sentence, indicate which use of the ablative case is illustrated by the italicized phrase.

(A) accompaniment   (B) agent   (C) manner   (D) means

1. _____ In Rome, the chief priestess of the Vestal Virgins lived *with seventeen other women* of various ages.

2. _____ They honored their patron goddess with a perpetual flame that they tended *with great enthusiasm.*

3. _____ Sometimes, however, a Vestal Virgin who failed in her duties was publicly chastened and afflicted *with a severe punishment.*

4. _____ Once, a priestess named Gabinia was *unjustly* accused and nearly died.

5. _____ Most Vestals, however, were greatly respected *by the Romans.*

Translate the italicized phrases from the preceding sentences.

6. _____

7. _____

8. _____

9. _____

10. _____

LESSON XXXVIII

VĒRUS RŌMĀNUS

 Vocabulary As you learn new vocabulary items, you will find that there are often multiple meanings for a word, including some that are not given in your book. Be attentive to new meanings, some of which may be connected with English derivatives of the word.

Modus, *manner,* for example, can also mean *limit* (as in English *moderation*) or *method.* Cf. English *modus operandi,* "method of operating."

Moneō, *warn,* can also mean *to advise.* Cf. English *monitor, admonition.*

Translate.

1. Our friendship is without limit.

_____

2. Who will advise you?

_____

Your expanded vocabulary will come to include many apparent synonyms. **Nam** and **prō,** for instance, both mean *for,* but the conjunction **nam** means *for* in the sense of *because* (cf. the conjunction **quod**). The preposition **prō** means *for* meaning *on behalf of.* Observe these differences in meaning and usage while translating the following sentences.

3. Rōmānī ōrāculum petīvērunt, <u>nam</u> Rōma in perīculō erat.

_____

_____

4. Marcus Curtius vītam <u>prō</u> patriā dōnāvit, nam Rōmam amāvit.

_____

The preposition **ob,** meaning *because of,* can also be translated *for.*

5. Ob animum Rōma Mārcum Curtium semper laudāvit.

_____

Name _____ Date _____

 B **Interrogative and relative pronouns** Because it is important to distinguish between inter-rogative and relative pronouns, mark with an X cases where the forms of the interrogative pronoun differ from the forms of the relative pronoun.

| | SINGULAR | | | | PLURAL | |
	MASCULINE	FEMININE	NEUTER	MASCULINE	FEMININE	NEUTER
NOMINATIVE	_____	_____	_____	_____	_____	_____
GENITIVE	_____	_____	_____	_____	_____	_____
DATIVE	_____	_____	_____	_____	_____	_____
ACCUSATIVE	_____	_____	_____	_____	_____	_____
ABLATIVE	_____	_____	_____	_____	_____	_____

In the sentences below, some italicized words are relative pronouns, and some are interroga-tive pronouns. Write "RP" or "IP" above the line to show which is which, then write in the correct case, number, and gender of the Latin pronoun in the blank below. Remember: Relative pronouns' genders and numbers are determined by their antecedent!

1. The Tarpeian Rock is named for a maiden *who* betrayed Rome.

_____

2. *Who* was this maiden?

_____

3. The temple, *which* stood on the Capitoline, was dedicated to Jupiter.

_____

4. *What* was the duty of the priest in this temple?

_____

Here is a summary of the differences in usage and form between relative and interrogative pronouns.

RELATIVE PRONOUNS (1 AND 3)

- Introduce *dependent* clauses
- Agree with antecedents in gender
- Used to relate information about an an antecedent person or thing (...who(m).../...which...)

INTERROGATIVE PRONOUNS (2 AND 4)

- Introduce *independent* clauses
- Have no expressed antecedents
- Used to ask about the identity of a person or thing: (who(m)? what?)

Name _____ Date _____

C **Interrogative pronouns** It is important to carefully identify the case, number, and gender of an interrogative pronoun before translating. Some forms have more than one identification. Be alert to these as you complete the following exercise on interrogative pronouns.

GENDER(S), NUMBER(S), CASES(S)　　　　MEANING(S)

1. quōs? _____　_____

2. quōcum? _____　_____

3. cui? _____　_____

4. quōrum? _____　_____

5. quae? _____　_____

6. cuius? _____　_____

7. quibus? _____　_____

8. quī? _____　_____

9. quid? _____　_____

10. quās? _____　_____

D **Interrogative pronouns vs. interrogative adjectives** The interrogative adjective, as you know, differs only occasionally from the forms of the interrogative pronoun. Most often you will need to rely on context to tell the difference between them.

Indicate whether each form is an interrogative pronoun, interrogative adjective, or either. No context is given, so you must rely solely on your knowledge of forms!

INTERROGATIVE PROUNOUN/ADJ./EITHER

1. quid ...? _____

2. quam ...? _____

3. quae ...? _____

4. quem ...? _____

5. quis ...? _____

6. quā ...? _____

7. cui...? _____

8. quod ...? _____

9. quī...? _____

10. quibus ...? _____

E **Interrogative pronoun vs. interrogative adjective** Translate each of the following questions, and then answer it in English, based on your knowledge of Greek and Roman gods and goddesses. Before beginning, mark each interrogative either IP (interrogative pronoun) or IA (interrogative adjective) so that you are clear on the difference.

Nota•Bene In English, the interrogative pronoun is always some form of *who?* or *what?* The interrogative adjective is *which x? what y,* NEVER a form of "who."

1. Quis est deus bellī?

   Translation: _____

   Answer: _____

2. Quis est dea frūmentī?

   Translation: _____

   Answer: _____

3. Quae dea est rēgīna deōrum?

   Translation: _____

   Answer: _____

4. Quī deus est dominus īnferōrum?

   Translation: _____

   Answer: _____

5. Quid est signum Neptūnī?

   Translation: _____

   Answer: _____

6. Quod signum ā Mercuriō portātur?

   Translation: _____

   Answer: _____

7. Quis ā Plūtōne amāta est?

   Translation: _____

   Answer: _____

8. Quid a deā Venere in Carthāgine effectum est?

   Translation: _____

   Answer: _____

9. Quōrum līberī erant Apollō et Diāna?

   Translation: _____

   Answer: _____

10. Ā quō Sāturnus ex Olympō excēdere coāctus est?

    Translation: _____

    Answer: _____

F **Interrogative pronoun vs. interrogative adjective** Indicate above each sentence whether the italicized word is an interrogative adjective (IA) or an interrogative pronoun (IP). Then translate the italicized word into Latin.

Nota•Bene Remember that an adjective will always agree with a noun in case, number, and gender. Thus, if the word *which* or *what* stands next to a noun and asks a question about it, it is an *adjective*. Make sure your Latin interrogative adjectives agree in case, number, and gender with these nouns!

1. *Who* was the father of Iulus?

_____

2. *Who* were his grandparents?

_____

Notice that the English word *who* is both singular and plural. As for the relative pronoun, Latin has separate singular and plural forms for interrogatives.

3. *What* Roman family traced its descent from Iulus?

_____

4. *What* was the town that he founded?

_____

5. *What* protection did the gods give to this city?

_____

LESSON XXXIX

PŪBLIUS PŪBLIAE SAL.

A **Vocabulary: prepositions** This lesson introduces two new prepositions, both of which govern the accusative case. Remember that it is important to know whether a preposition's objects are ablative or accusative. It is also important to know how the few prepositions that govern both cases differ accordingly in translation. So, let's review.

Translate each phrase, in more than one way if asked.

1–2. ā deō *(translate two ways)* _____

_____

3–4. ad magistrum *(translate two ways)* _____

_____

5. cum poētis _____

6. cum beneficiō _____

7–8. de Vesuviō *(translate two ways)* _____

_____

9. ē locō _____

10–11. in librō *(translate two ways)* _____

_____

12. in templa _____

13. in Aegyptōs _____

14. inter viās _____

15. ob concordiam _____

16. per oppida _____

17. sine amīcīs _____

18. sub portam _____

19. sub undīs _____

20. trāns agrōs _____

Name _____ Date _____

SCHOOLS, SITES, AND SIGHTS IN THE ROMAN EMPIRE

UNIT VII REVIEW

 Derivatives

1. Identify the Latin verb from which each of the italicized words is derived.

2. Define these English derivatives using the meaning of their Latin root. (This isn't always easy; consult a dictionary if needed.)

1. The Philippines, *ceded* by Spain to the U.S., is now an independent nation.

   _____

2. Some metals, like gold, are more *ductile* than others.

   _____

3. The *gestation* period of marsupials is shorter than that of other mammals.

   _____

4. The official papers *submitted* to the consul were carefully presented to the foreign ambassador.

   _____

5. Most found the instructor quite able to *explicate* the more difficult texts assigned.

   _____

6. The lawyer's *cogent* argument persuaded the jury.

   _____

7. He worked with the project from its *inceptive* stage.

   _____

8. His eyes took on a *concupiscent* glow as he looked at the shiny new car.

   _____

9. The *fugitive* light of evening swiftly gave way to darkness.

   _____

10. The judge's *interdiction* prevented the law from going into effect.

    _____

11. The *intermittent* rain caused delays in the tournament.

    _____

12. This attorney made a *cogent* argument for the suspect's release on bail.

    _____

13. The teacher tried to help the *scribbling* child to be more accurate.

_____

14. While working at the *conservatory* the director experienced few interruptions.

_____

15. Many organizations focus on developing *self-sustaining* modes of production.

_____

16. The *petitionary* felon did not escape his sentence.

_____

17. The theory *posited* by the archaeologist was based on objects discovered in Crete.

_____

18. The young Narcissus was *susceptible* to admiring his own appearance.

_____

19. The mule is not a *tractable* beast.

_____

20. The book outlined the *antecedents* of Mussolini's rise to power in Italy.

_____

B **Grammar review: relative pronoun forms** Translate *only* the relative pronouns in the following sentences. Consider carefully their antecedents and context before choosing the form.

1. Have you heard about the first war at Troy, *which* precedes the famous ten year siege?

_____

2. Laomedon, an early king, *who* was helped by Apollo and Neptune, had built the first walls around the city.

_____

3. Later, however, he tried to cheat the gods, *to whom* he had promised a reward.

_____

4. As punishment, Neptune sent a sea monster* *which* Laomedon destroyed with the help of Hercules.

_____

*mōnstrum, -ī, n.

5. In return, the king promised white horses to Hercules, but again he did not honor the words *that* he had spoken.

_____

6. Hercules therefore gathered troops* in Greece, *with whom* he sailed to Troy.

6. Hercules therefore gathered troops* in Greece, *with whom* he sailed to Troy.

_____

cōpiae, -ārum, f.

7. Breaching the walls at a weak spot, he killed Laomedon and his sons, *by whom* the agreement had been broken.

_____

8. One son of Laomedon, *who* was named Podarces, was spared by the embittered Hercules.

_____

[Podarces was renamed Priam. After his release, he became the king of Troy.]

9. The hero knew that this prince alone had tried to make Laomedon give up the horses *which* he had promised.

_____

10. The very walls* *whose* construction gave rise to this trouble were later breached to admit the Trojan Horse.

_____

mūrus, -ī m.

UNIT VIII

ADVENTURES ABROAD AND LIFE AT HOME

LESSON XL

ULIXĒS

A Vocabulary Two of the nouns in this lesson, **dux** and **lēx,** are related to verbs that you already know. Be careful not to confuse parts of speech as you translate. Remember that context, word form, and (sometimes) word order are the best indicators of grammatical function.

Translate each of the following sentences completely, paying particular attention to the forms of the italicized words.

1. Officium *ducis* dūcere est.

_____

2. Caesar, nōs ad glōriam *dūcis.*

_____

3. *Lege* bona exempla, fīlī mī.

_____

4. Dē *lēge* novā lēgimus.

_____

B Third declension: base and case endings You will recall that most words of the first and second declensions show the same base in their nominative singular and their genitive singular forms. It would seem, therefore, that the base could be derived from either form.

You have understood for some time, however, that with nouns like **ager** and **magister** (or adjectives like **noster** and **sacer**), it is necessary to use the genitive singular form of a dictionary entry to derive the base.

Have you read pages 280–282?

In the third declension, you should always learn the genitive because the nominative singular alone cannot supply the base that you need to spell the other forms.

Complete the following.

	GENITIVE SINGULAR	BASE
1. fāma	_____	_____
2. deus	_____	_____
3. verbum	_____	_____

4. puer   _____   _____

5. ager   _____   _____

6. salūs   _____   _____

You have already been introduced to some endings of the third declension.

In addition, you already know that **-ī** can be a dative singular ending (as in **cui***), and you have already encountered **-ibus,** the common ending of the dative and ablative plural for all three genders of the third declension (remember **quibus?**).

Furthermore, the genitive plural ending **-um** is part of the other genitive plural endings you have memorized.

Remember that the genitive singular ending **-is** must be distinguished from **-īs,** the dative and ablative plural ending of first and second declension nouns.

Identify the declension, case(s), and number(s) of each noun.

	DECLENSION	CASE	NUMBER
7. equī	_____	_____	_____
8. ducī	_____	_____	_____
9. dominus	_____	_____	_____
10. hominibus	_____	_____	_____
11. salūte	_____	_____	_____
12. serve	_____	_____	_____
13. lēgum	_____	_____	_____
14. signum	_____	_____	_____

C **Adjective agreement with nouns of the third declension** Adjectives, in other words, of the first and second declension do not change their endings to third declension if they modufy nouns of the third declension. The adjectives that you know agree with third declension nouns in case, number, and gender, even though their endings are those of the first and second declension.

Circle the first or second declension adjective that agrees in case, number, and gender with each third declension noun.

1. ducem

   a. clārus   **b.** clāram   **c.** clārum   **d.** clārōrum

2. pāce

   a. aequē   **b.** aequā   **c.** aequō   **d.** aequa

3. lēgēs

   a. sacrī   **b.** sacrae   **c.** sacrōs   **d.** sacrīs

4. salūs

   a. ēgregius   **b.** ēgregiōs   **c.** ēgregia   **d.** ēgregiās

5. hominī

   a. reliquī   **b.** reliquus   **c.** reliquō   **d.** reliquīs

Name _____ Date _____

Circle all the nouns in each set that agree with the given adjective.

6. paucīs

   a. mīlitis   **b.** mīlitibus   **c.** mīlitēs   **d.** mīlitī

7. firmae

   a. pācis   **b.** pācēs   **c.** pāx   **d.** pācī

8. bonī

   a. dux   **b.** ducēs   **c.** duce   **d.** ducis

9. miserō

   a. hominī   **b.** homō   **c.** homine   **d.** hominis

10. prīmās

   a. lēgēs   **b.** lēgis   **c.** lēgibus   **d.** lēgem

 Third declension: gender The first declension, as you know, contains nouns of two genders: masculine and feminine. However, the second declension contains nouns of all three genders.

The third declension is the largest declension. It contains many nouns of all three genders. Interestingly enough, the masculine and feminine case endings of this group are identical.

Consider each pair of nouns carefully, and indicate with an X what the given nouns have in common.

	DECLENSION	GENDER	DECLENSION & GENDER
1. puella; poēta			
2. poēta; populus			
3. populus; puer			
4. puer; pater			
5. pater; frāter			
6. frāter; māter			
7. māter; familia			
8. familia; fīlia			
9. fīlia; soror			
10. soror; puella			

Name _____ Date _____

 Three declensions: case identification In each of the following groups, there are two nouns that belong to the given case and two that do not. Circle the nouns that belong to the given case.

NOMINATIVE	mīles	hominī	magister	discipulīs
GENITIVE	nautīs	lēgis	pācī	grātiae
DATIVE	mīlitibus	servō	homō	colōnī
ACCUSATIVE	lēgum	officia	rēgem	salūs
ABLATIVE	amīce	cibus	mīlite	ducibus

LESSON XLI

COLŌNĪ

A **Nota•Bene**   The principal parts of **stō** are not as regular as those of most other verbs in the first conjugation (such as **trānsportō**). Compare the verb **dō**.

dō	**dare**	**dedī**	**datus**
stō	**stāre**	**stetī**	**stātūrus**

There are many good English derivatives of **stō**. Choose the correct answer.

1. That theory has been fully _____, for it *stands up* under close scrutiny.

   a. predestined   **b.** reinstated   **c.** resisted   **d.** substantiated

2. Since most of us lead very busy lives, we often buy _____ foods; they *stand* ready for quick preparation and consumption.

   a. constant   **b.** instant   **c.** obstinate   **d.** static

3. The _____ of a storm is measured by the time that *stands between* the flash of lightning and the sound of thunder.

   a. constituency   **b.** distance   **c.** existence   **d.** stance

4. The _____ cough *stood* in the way of my cheering for our team.

   a. constant   **b.** insubstantial   **c.** stable   **d.** statutory

5. Students are well-advised to *stand off* from offers of illegal drugs; they should "Just Say No," or _____.

   a. assist   **b.** consist   **c.** desist   **d.** subsist

B **Verb forms: 4th conjugation** Circle the correct answer.

1. Which of the following is imperative?

   a. venī   **b.** vēnī

2. Which of the following is a participle?

   a. invēnī   **b.** inventī

3. Which of the following is passive?

   a. audiēris   **b.** audīveris

4. What tense is each of the verbs in the preceding question?

   _____   _____

5. Which of the following is a present passive infinitive?

   a. convēnī   **b.** convenīrī

C **Review of case endings** Circle the correct answer.

1. Which two of the following forms are nominative?

   a. homō   **b.** colōnō   **c.** lēgis   **d.** elūdus

2. Which two of the following forms are genitive?

   a. oppidum   **b.** ducis   **c.** mīlitum   **d.** ōtiīs

3. Which two of the following forms are dative?

   a. hominibus   **b.** salūtis   **c.** cibus   **d.** nūntiīs

4. Which two of the following forms are accusative?

   a. sententiārum   **b.** silvam   **c.** ducum   **d.** lēgem

5. Which two of the following forms are ablative?

   a. armīs   **b.** pācis   **c.** mīlite   **d.** domine

D **Review of ablatives** Express the following in Latin.

1. by the leader (*ablative of agent*)

   _____

2. with the soldiers (*ablative of accompaniment*)

   _____

3. very safely (*ablative of manner*)

   _____

4. with laws (*ablative of means*)

   _____

5. concerning peace (*object of preposition*)

   _____

E **Review of verb tenses and voice** For each verb, identify the conjugation, tense, voice, and stem from which it is formed. Then translate in the space provided.

	CONJUGATION	TENSE	VOICE	STEM
1. premis	_____	_____	_____	_____
2. monitus eris	_____	_____	_____	_____
3. relinquēminī	_____	_____	_____	_____

	CONJUGATION	TENSE	VOICE	STEM
4. conveniēbātis	_____	_____	_____	_____
	_____			
5. fugiunt	_____	_____	_____	_____
	_____			
6. remānserat	_____	_____	_____	_____
	_____			
7. stābimus	_____	_____	_____	_____
	_____			
8. audiar	_____	_____	_____	_____
	_____			
9. incepta erant	_____	_____	_____	_____
	_____			
10. clāmātum est	_____	_____	_____	_____
	_____			

LESSON XLII

PLĪNIUS ET PUER

 A **Words used as nouns** What is the name for an adjective or verbal form used as a noun?

_____

 B **Perfect passive participle: use as noun** Look at these forms which are good examples of what you have named above. Match each word to its meaning.

1. _____ actum
2. _____ datum
3. _____ dēbitum
4. _____ iussum
5. _____ mandātum
6. _____ meritum
7. _____ monitum
8. _____ rēctum
9. _____ scrīptum
10. _____ vīsum

a. something charged or commissioned
b. something advised
c. something ordered or appointed
d. something given
e. something done
f. something guided or set right
g. something owed
h. something seen
i. something deserved
j. something written

 C **Compounds of sum** You have learned that **sum,** like other verbs, has compounds, e.g. **absum** *(be absent)* and **adsum** *(be present).* A third compound is introduced in this lesson. It uses the root **pos-, pot-** and means *to be able.* There are no passive forms for any of these compounds. **Possum** is often translated with the English auxiliaries *can* or *could.* However, since Latin does not often use auxiliary verbs, **possum** will function as a main verb. As such, it almost always requires a complementary infinitive. I can swim = I am able <u>to swim</u>.

Have you read page 290?

You now know three compounds of the linking verb **sum.** There are others that are also created from prepositions used as prefixes. These are the most common compounds.

dēsum	*fall short, fail (be missing from)*
intersum	*take part in (be among)*
praesum	*be in charge (be at the head of)*
prōsum	*be of use (be for)*
supersum	*survive (be left over)*

Choose the correct answer to each question, and then translate the four verbs.

1. Which of the following is present?

    a. sumus   **b.** aberit   **c.** adfuit   **d.** poterant

    _____   _____   _____   _____

2. Which is the following is perfect?

    a. fueris   **b.** āfuērunt   **c.** ades   **d.** potuerātis

    _____   _____   _____   _____

3. Which of the following is future?

    a. erātis   **b.** adfueram   **c.** aderam   **d.** poterō

    _____   _____   _____   _____

4. Which of the following is imperfect?

    a. dēfuerat   **b.** eram   **c.** potuistī   **d.** adsunt

    _____   _____   _____   _____

5. Which of the following is future perfect?

    a. eritis   **b.** aberimus   **c.** interfuērunt   **d.** potuerit

    _____   _____   _____   _____

D   **Irregular verb possum** Translate the following, paying careful attention to tense.

1. I was able _____

2. you *(pl.)* could _____

3. you *(sing.)* will have been able _____

4. she will be able _____

5. he had been able _____

6. he was able _____

7. they can _____

8. we could _____

9. I am able _____

10. they have been able _____

Name _____ Date _____

 Forms of sum and possum The following fictional memoir pertains to Roman politics. You will create synopses of **sum** and **possum** as you translate the italicized words.

1. *I am* a **consul,** one of the Roman states' two chief officers. As such, *I can* call meetings of the Roman senate and carry out its decisions. My very title is derived from my obtaining the counsel of the senate and carrying out its decrees.

   _____   _____

2. *I have been* a public official since I was 31, the earliest age to be elected **quaestor.** Each consul, provincial governor, and general has a **quaestor** who handles his financial affairs, but, more importantly, since that point in my life *I have been* able to pursue the **cursus honorum.**

   _____   _____

3. During my quaestorship, I thought: "With luck, I will be elected at 37 to the office of **aedile,** and *I will be* very much in the public eye since *I will be able* to present athletic games for the people to enjoy." I knew, of course, that my other duties would include caring for the streets, markets, and food supply, all of which are also matters of great importance to the Roman people.

   _____   _____

4. For many years *I was* hopeful that one day I would become **praetor,** and at 40—the earliest possible year—I became one! In that position, *I was able* to make judicial decisions. The law, which is the strong foundation of our Republic, has always attracted me.

   _____   _____

5. Even before my election to the consulship which I now hold, as **praetor** *I had been,* so to speak, a **consul** from time to time, for in the absence of the men who were then **consuls** *I had been able* to act for the senate.

   _____   _____

6. Rumor has it that my next appointment will be that of governor (prōconsul) to Spain. In a little more than a year's time, therefore, *I will have been* in government service for more than a decade. By the end of my career in politics, therefore, *I will have been able* to serve my country in many ways.

   _____   _____

LESSON XLIII

PŪBLIA PŪBLIŌ SAL.

 A **Vocabulary: words frequently confused** Now that your vocabulary includes at least three hundred Latin words, you have observed that words like **amō** and **amīcus**, though different parts of speech, are closely related both in meaning and spelling.

EXEMPLĪ GRĀTIĀ

Nūntius properat.	*The messenger is hurrying.*
Victōriam nūntiābit.	*He will announce a victory.*

Translate the following.

1. Pugna in Graeciā intermissa est.

_____

_____

2. Rōmānī ibi magnō cum animō pugnāvērunt.

_____

3. Servī nunc līberābuntur.

_____

4. Lībertus* semper amīcitiam cum dominō cuius servus fuit servābit.

_____

*a freed man

5. Dux magnus Scīpiō in Āfricā bellum gessit.

_____

6. In Carthāginiēnsēs virōs dūxit.

_____

7. Fugite ā perīculō!

_____

8. Fuga longa et dūra erit.

_____

9. Rēgēs aequē, fīlia mea.

_____

10. Rēgēs in Americā nōn sunt.

_____

B **Perfect passive participle** Supply an appropriate Latin participle for the italicized words in each sentence. Remember that the case of the word that you supply must agree with some the word it modifies in each sentence.

1. After the death of King Odaenathus, the Palmyrans, *led* by his widow Zenobia, threw off the yoke of imperial Rome.

   _____

2. *Influenced* by a desire to equal Cleopatra, Queen Zenobia marched against the Roman garrisons in Africa.

   _____

3. Roman soldiers, *led out* by Aurelian, moved to check her advances.

   _____

4. *Led back* to Rome in defeat, Zenobia called for golden chains.

   _____

5. *Led across* the Forum in Aurelian's triumph, this prisoner impressed Rome with her queenly bearing.

   _____

LESSON XLIV

CIRCĒ

 A **Vocabulary** In the vocabulary for this lesson, there is a word that has a special plural meaning. Let's review other nouns that also have unusual plural forms. Define each.

DEFINITIONS

1. impedīmenta _____

2. studia _____

3. loca _____

4. litterae _____

 B **Ablative absolute construction** Have you read pages 299–300? As you know, the ablative case (with or without prepositions) is used to express adverbial ideas such as:

With what?	**armīs** *(means)*	
How?	**cum animō** *(manner)*	
When?	**annō Dominī** *(time when)*	
Where?	**in agrō** *(place where)*	

There are also adverbial clauses in Latin such as:

quod cōnsultus erat	*because he had been consulted*
ubi stābant	*where they were standing*
nam praedam relīquērunt	*for they have left the loot*

However, these clauses are often replaced by the special use of the ablative case called the *ablative absolute.*

Like most of the special constructions you have learned so far, the ablative absolute has certain distinctive characteristics. Look for the following:

• a noun or a pronoun in the ablative case

• a perfect passive participle, which is also in the ablative case since it is used as a modifier

• the endings: **-a, -o, -is**

• an ablative phrase that begins a Latin sentence; regardless of its position, it is almost always set off by commas

Since the ablative absolute can be used to show cause or time, your translations may sometimes require one of these conjuctions. Practice these and more flexible translations in answering the following questions.

1. Why was Polyphemus so angry?
   Graecīs in spēluncā* vīsīs...

   _____

   *spēlunca, -ae, f. *cave*

2. When did Ulysses' men forget their homeland?
   Lōtō acceptā et ēsā*...

   _____

   * edō, edere, edī, esus, *eat*. Lōtus, although second declension, is feminine in gender.

3. Under what circumstances did Mercury tell Ulysses that he would be able to rescue his crew?
   Rēgīnā herbā territā...

   _____

4. Why was Eurylochous alarmed?
   Sociīs in animālia versīs...

   _____

5. When did Ulysses return to the island of Aeolia?
   Ventīs acceptīs āb Aeolō amissīs...

   _____

Participial phrases Now that you are reading about Ulysses, you may enjoy knowing more about the background of his story. As you translate each sentence, try to achieve some variety in the English that you use to render the participles.

Long before the chiefs of Greece brought war against Troy, Ulysses sought to marry an incomparably beautiful princess named Helen. He was only one of many famous suitors, however, and showed great wisdom as the rivalry for her hand intensified.

1. Cōnsultus ā ducibus reliquīs, Ulixēs verba fēcit.

   _____

2. Adductī verbīs Ulixis, ducēs cōnsilium cepērunt.

   _____

They agreed to set aside their rivalry as soon as Helen had declared her choice. They would thereafter support both Helen and the man she selected.

3. "Causa virī ā Helenā lectī semper ā nōbīs sustinēbitur."

   _____

4. "Concordiam ita effectam dēfendēmus."

   _____

5. Helenā captā ad Troiam et trānsportātā, bellum in Troiānōs ā Graecīs nūntiātum est.

   _____

6. Ulixēs, fāmā dē bellō audītā, pugnāre nōn cupīvit et esse insānus sīmulāvit.*

_____

_____

_____

pretended

This ruse was uncovered, however, and Ulysses was persuaded to join his fellow Greeks in the mission of honor to which they had all pledged themselves.

7. Officiō susceptō, ad locum ubi Achillēs habitābat Ulixēs missus est.

_____

_____

_____

8. Achille petītō inventōque, Ulixēs ad Aulem* processit et nāvigāre ad Troiam cum reliquīs parāvit.

_____

_____

_____

Aulis, a seaport

9. Decem annīs ad Troiam actīs, Ulixēs sociusque clāram statuam Minervae ē templō Troiānō remōvērunt.

_____

_____

_____

10. Īrā* Troiānōrum incitātā, Ulixēs cum sociīs parāvērunt equum quī signum pācis vīsus est sed vērē māchina bellī erat.

_____

_____

_____

*īra, -ae, f. *anger, wrath*

ADVENTURES ABROAD AND LIFE AT HOME

UNIT VIII REVIEW

 Latin words in European languages The following columns contain words from five modern languages. Upon occasion, your textbook has referred to these languages by a special name that they share as a group. What is that name?

_____

To better appreciate the lists of words, first translate the list of English words into Latin. Then use the answers to identify the meanings of the European derivatives.

daughter	_____	much	_____
day	_____	night	_____
do, make	_____	read	_____
eye	oculus, -ī, m. _____	sea	_____
foot	_____	son	_____
give	_____	space	_____
god	_____	time	_____
high	_____	water	_____
I	_____	who	_____
man, human	_____	write	_____

Name _____ Date _____

Now use the answers to clarify the meanings of the Romance derivatives.

Portuguese	Spanish	French	Italian	Romanian	English
o dia	el día	le jour	il giorno	ziua	_____
a noite	la noche	la nuit	la notteno	aptea	_____
o pé	el pie	le pied	il piede	piciorul	_____
o olho	el ojo	l'oeil	l'occhio	ochiul	_____
dar	dar	donner	dare	da	_____
fazer	hacer	faire	fare	face	_____
ler	leer	lire	leggere	citi	_____
escrever	escribir	écrire	scrivere	scrie	_____
a filha	la hija	la fille	la figlia	fiica	_____
o filho	el hijo	le fils	il figlio	fiul	_____
alto	alto	haut(e)	alto	inalt	_____
muito	mucho	beaucoup	molto	mult	_____
a agua	el agua	l'eau	l'acqua	apa	_____
o mar	el mar	la mer	il mare	marea	_____
o tempo	el tiempo	le temps	il tempo	timpul	_____
o espaço	el espacio	l'espace	il spazio	spatiu	_____
eu	yo	je	io	eu	_____
quem	quien	qui	chi	cine	_____
o homem	el hombre	l'homme	l'uomo	omul	_____
o deus	el dios	le dieu	il dio	dumnezeu	_____

Name _____ Date _____

THE ADVENTURES OF ULYSSES, ROMULUS, REMUS, AND PYRRHUS

SĪRĒNĒS ET PHAEĀCIA

 A **Neuter nouns of the third declension** The neuter nouns introduced in this lesson demonstrate a pattern that will help you to learn the genitive singular forms of other neuter nouns.

Compare:

> **flūmen, flūminis**
> **nōmen, nōminis**

1. Based on this pattern, what would be the genitive singular of **ōmen** *(omen, augury)*?

_____

2. What would be the genitive singular of **lūmen** *(light, lamp)*?

_____

Compare:

> **corpus, corporis**
> **tempus, temporis**

3. What would be the nominative and accusative forms of a neuter noun whose genitive singular is **lītoris** *(shore)*?

_____

4. What would be the genitive singular of the third declension neuter noun **pectus** *(chest)*?

_____

Note that even the gender and genitive singular of masculine nouns like **ōrdō, ōrdinis, cardō, cardinis** *(hinge),* can be more easily remembered by mentally associating them with another masculine noun like **homō, hominis.**

5. How would you say in Latin, the shape of the hinge?

_____

Ōrdō, by the way, refers to rank, as in the ordinal numbers (**prīmus, secundus, tertius,** etc.) It does not refer to the kind of order that is a command (**mandātum**) or an instruction (**iussum.**)

B **Neuter nouns of the third declension** Have you noticed that the genitive singular ending of third declension neuter nouns is the same as the corresponding case endings of nouns like **mīles** or **lēx?** Mark with an X other endings of the third declension that are the same as those of **mīles** or **lēx.**

	SINGULAR	PLURAL
NOMINATIVE	_____	_____
GENITIVE	_____	_____
DATIVE	_____	_____
ACCUSATIVE	_____	_____
ABLATIVE	_____	_____

1. Which endings were not marked?

_____

2. Note that these endings illustrate the *neuter law* that you learned in Unit III. Restate this law.

_____

_____

Note also that the plural case endings of these neuter nouns in the nominative and accusative are just like the corresponding case endings of the second declension (**-a.**)

Identify the case of each italicized word and then translate each sentence.

3. *Nōmina* prīmōrum et ultimōrum* rēgnum Rōmae erant Rōmulus et Tarquinius Superbus.

_____

_____

*ultimus, -a, -um: last

4. Nōvistīne *nōmina* relīquōrum rēgum Rōmae?

_____

5. *Exempla* factōrum Rōmulī et reliquōrum rēgum in litterīs* Rōmānīs cōnservāta sunt.

_____

_____

*Even today, literature is often to referred to as *letters*. Some universities have a *College of Arts and Letters.*

6. *Exempla* et bonōrum et malōrum rēgum memoriā tenēre dēbēmus.

_____

7. In which of the preceding sentences are the italicized words nominative ?

_____

8. In which of the preceding sentences are the italicized words accusative?

_____

Name _____ Date _____

C **Case identification** Circle an appropriate response to each question.

1. Which of the following is not neuter?

   a. capita   **b.** facta   **c.** fuga   **d.** perīcula   **e.** nōmina

   2. Which of the following is not genitive?

   a. cūrārum   **b.** regnīs   **c.** modōrum   **d.** vulneris   **e.** sorōrum

   3. Which of the following is not accusative?

   a. vulnera   **b.** prōvinciam   **c.** studium   **d.** tempus   **e.** flūminum

   4. Which of the following is not singular?

   a. capita   **b.** hominem   **c.** lūdum   **d.** mīles   **e.** carmen

   5. Which of the following is not plural?

   a. corpora   **b.** pedum   **c.** rēgna   **d.** impedīmentum   **e.** ōrdinum

D **Neuter nouns of the third declension** Translate the italicized words in each sentence with careful attention to its function in the sentence.

1. The *head* of the god Janus was remarkable; it faced in two directions.

   _____

2. *Heads* of Janus appeared on many ancient coins.

   _____

   (Romans used coins to play a guessing game called **capita aut nāvēs.** To what modern game does this correspond?)

3. The spirit *of the River* Tiber is personified in art and literature as an old man.

   _____

4. The gods *of* other *rivers* are also depicted in this way.

   _____

5. A Roman gave *the name* of his **genius locī** special honor.

   _____

6. Roman families made offerings *to the names* of their household gods.

   _____

7. The letters *A.U.C.* refer to the way that the Romans reckoned *time* from the founding of their city.

   _____

8. Julius Caesar commissioned Egyptian astronomers to regulate *the times** of the months.

   _____

   *The word **tempus** can refer to units of time.

9. The mighty Achilles was slain *by a wound* to his heel.

_____

10. Jason, protected by a magic potion, emerged *without wounds* from his encounter with the fire-breathing bulls.

_____

E **Sentences with participles** Note that in the following sentences about the *Odyssey*, the participles are nominative because they modify subjects that are expressed by the personal endings of the verbs.

After you translate each sentence, identify the character to whom each refers.

a. Aeolus	**f.** Eurylochus
b. Alcinous	**g.** Mercurius
c. amicae Nausicaae	**h.** nautae Ulixis
d. Calypso	**i.** Polyphēmus
e. Circē	**j.** Ulixes

1. _____ Ligātus ad nāvem, Sīrēnēs audīre poterat sed carminibus eōrum in perīculum nōn trāctus est.

_____

_____

2. _____ Vulnerātus ā Graecīs, eōs invenīre et interficere nōn poterat.

_____

3. _____ Territae ā barbarō, lūdum intermīsērunt.

_____

4. _____ Inventus cōnsultusque dē rēgīnā inimīcā, Ulixī herbam magicam dedit.

_____

5. _____ Petītus rogātusque dē ventīs āmissīs, nōn iam amīcus Graecīs erat.

_____

6. _____ Adductī lōtō sed nōn relictī ā sociīs, ad nāvēs redāctī sunt.

_____

7. _____ Nōn versus in animal, ad Ulixem fūgit.

_____

8. _____ Retenta coāctaque herbā, virōs līberāvit ē fōrmīs animalium in quibus tentī erant.

_____

9. _____ Iussa nōn Ulixem retinēre, nāvem prō Graecīs parāvit.

_____

10. _____ Ob auxilium Ulixī datum, affectus poenā ā Neptūnō nōn iam ā Phaeāciā nāvigāre poterat.

_____

LESSON XLVI

PĒNELOPĒ

 Third declension *i*-stem nouns The declension of i-stem nouns described in this lesson does not differ greatly from the other nouns of the third declension. As you can see, the primary distinctions of this group are: 1) the genitive plural ending (**-ium** for **-um**) for all genders; 2) the nominative and accusative plural endings of neuter nouns (**-ia** for **-a**), and 3) the ablative singular of these same neuter nouns (**-ī** for **-e**).

 The *i*-stem endings of the third declension are extremely important because you will soon be learning third declension adjectives, all of which follow the declension of *i*-stem nouns.

Remember that i-stem nouns usually have 1) a base ending in two consonants (e.g., **mōns, mōntis**, m.) or have 2) equal number of syllables in the nominative and genitive singular (e.g., **cī-vis, cī-vis**, m./f.). Which of the following must be *i*-stems? Place a check beside those that qualify.

1. _____ **sōl, sōlis**, m., *sun*
2. _____ **ignis, ignis**, m., *fire*
3. _____ **lapis, lapidis**, m., *stone*
4. _____ **pānis, pānis**, m., *bread*
5. _____ **fōns, fontis**, m., *fountain*
6. _____ **fēlēs, fēlis**, f., *cat*
7. _____ **bōs, bovis**, m. and f., *cow*
8. _____ **plēbs, plēbis**, f., *the common people*
9. _____ **frōns, frondis**, f., *foliage*
10. _____ **quiēs, quiētis**, f., *rest*

B **Case identification.** Identify the case(s) of each Latin word.

1. monte _____
2. mare _____
3. corpus _____
4. vestibus _____
5. iter _____
6. fīnēs _____
7. capita _____

8. maria _____

9. itinerum _____

10. nāvium _____

Prepositions and case usage Translate each phrase with attention to the case that must be used with each preposition.

1. near the ship

   _____

2. down from the mountain

   _____

3. on the sea

   _____

4. by an enemy

   _____

5. without borders

   _____

6. on account of the harmony of the citizens

   _____

7. through the waves of the sea

   _____

8. before the time of the kings

   _____

9. across a number of rivers

   _____

10. into the territory of the enemy

    _____

   (Remember that both Latin nouns in this phrase are plural in Latin, even though they are singular in English.)

Name _____ Date _____

LESSON XLVII

FĪNIS LABŌRUM

 A **Third declension adjectives** In this lesson you are introduced to a second group of adjectives—adjectives of the third declension. The adjectives you have been using until now had the endings of the first and second declensions. <u>These new adjectives are all i-stem, third declension in their case endings</u>.

However, adjectives of the third declension may differ in the number of nominative forms—some have one, some two, and a few have three nominative forms—one for each gender.

Which third declension adjective endings express the following:

1. The genitive singular for all three genders?

   _____

2. The dative and ablative plural forms of all three genders?

   _____

3. The genitive plural forms of all three genders?

   _____

4. The dative and ablative singular forms of all three genders?

   _____

B **Adjective/noun agreement** Post the following nouns beside the form of **omnis** that is identical in case, number, and gender. Some of the nouns will appear to qualify for placement in more than one position, so be sure to think carefully about the possibilities for each word. Use a pencil in case you need to erase.

arma	flūmina	locus	mīlitis	pede	undīs
capite	hominēs	magistrī	montium	puerō	verbum
causās	hostibus	māteriae	nōminī	sociīs	via
cūrā	lēgum	mātrī	officiōrum	sorōribus	virum
exemplī	linguam	memoriae	oppidīs	tempus	vulneribus

	MASCULINE	SINGULAR FEMININE	NEUTER
NOMINATIVE	omnis _____	omnis _____	omnis _____
genitive	omnis _____	omnis _____	omnis _____
DATIVE	omnī _____	omnī _____	omnī _____
ACCUSATIVE	omnem _____	omnem _____	omne _____
ABLATIVE	omnī _____	omnī _____	omnī _____

	MASCULINE	PLURAL FEMININE	NEUTER
NOMINATIVE	omnēs _____	omnēs _____	omnia _____
GENITIVE	omnium _____	omnium _____	omnium _____
DATIVE	omnibus _____	omnibus _____	omnibus _____
ACCUSATIVE	omnēs _____	omnēs _____	omnia _____
ABLATIVE	omnibus _____	omnibus _____	omnibus _____

C **Adjectives of three declensions** In each sentence, replace the italicized Latin adjective of the third declension with a corresponding form of the adjective requested in parentheses. Be sure it agrees in case, number, and gender. Be prepared to translate both versions orally.

1. *Celere* iter faciēmus.
   (Replace with a form of the adjective meaning *long*.)

   _____

2. Mīlitēs *fortēs* ad Asiam missī sunt.
   (Replace with a form of the adjective meaning *remaining*.)

   _____

3. Animalia lēgibus *nātūrālibus* reguntur.
   (Replace with a form of the adjective meaning *few*.)

   _____

4. Iūra servī et dominī nōn erant *paria*.
   (Replace with a form of the adjective meaning *just*.)

   _____

5. Nōn *omnēs* rēgēs Rōmae erant Etruscī.
   (Replace with a form of the adjective meaning *many*.)

   _____

D **Review of ablative absolute** The following sentences provide more practice with the ablative absolute construction you learned in Lesson XLIV. Answer each question by translating the Latin participial phrase as a subordinate clause *(when, since, although, if, etc.).*

1. Under what condition did Penelope say she would choose a new spouse?
   Meritō armīs rēgis mōnstrātō...

   _____

2. When did Ulysses' dog Argus die?
   Dominō cognitō...

   _____

3. When did Ulysses have to leave Calypso?
   Septem annīs in īnsulā āctīs...

   _____

4. Why did Neptune punish the Phaeacians?
   Auxiliō Graecīs ā rēge submissō...

   _____

5. When did the elderly Eumaeus and his young master Telemachus come to the aid of
   Ulysses?
   Pugnā in procōs* inceptā...

   _____

*proci, procōrum, m. *suitors*

LESSON XLVIII

RŌMULUS ET REMUS

 Vocabulary Read each sentence, and decide which given definition best translates the italicized word.

gerō   *to wage; to wear*

1. Ducēs quī bellum ēgregiē *gerēbant* in triumphīs dūcēbantur.

   _____

2. In triumphō, dux victōriōsus togam pictam* *gerēbat*.

   _____

   *embroidered

iter   *a journey; a route*

3. Orpheus *iter* ad īnferōs invēnit.

   _____

4. Uxōre receptā, Orpheus ex Erebō properāvit, sed in mediō *itinere* dubitāvit.

   _____

rēgnum   *kingdom, kingly power*

5. Ā tempore Rōmulī ad CCXLV A.U.C. *rēgnum* Rōmānum in quō multī populī continēbantur valēbat.

   _____

6. Fascēs erant signa *rēgnī*.

   _____

altus   *deep; high* (As a substantive, **altum** can mean either *depth* or *height*.)

7. In *altō* Iūppiter habitat.

   _____

8. In *altō* Neptūnus habitat.

   _____

aequus   *calm, just*

9. Lēgēs aequae populō grātae sunt.

   _____

10. Iniūriīs affectus, populus nōn *aequus* erit.

   _____

sub   *close to; under*

11. Caesar *sub* grātiā Fortūnae pugnāvit.

_____

12. Caesar mīlitēs castra pōnere *sub* flūmine Rhodānō iussit.

_____

dē   *about; [down] from*

13. Quid *dē* mathēmaticā nōvistī?

_____

14. Suntne trēs subtractī *dē* trīgintā XXVII aut CCXCVII?

_____

cōgō   *collect, compel*

15. Ex omnibus terrīs maribusque Aeolus ventōs *cōgēbat*.

_____

16. In spēluncā eōs remanēre *coēgit*.

_____

addūcō   *lead toward; influence*

17. Apolline duce, Mūsae ad montem sacram* *adductae* sunt.

_____

*Mt. Parnassus

18. Poētae ā Mūsīs *addūcuntur*.

_____

Vocabulary The following Latin nouns, all based on verbal roots, are names of roles and professions. Use your knowledge of the root meanings to match the words to their definitions.

1. ___ acceptor
2. ___ agitātor
3. ___ audītor
4. ___ clamātor
5. ___ consultor
6. ___ conservātor
7. ___ dator
8. ___ dēbitor
9. ___ dēfensor
10. ___ doctor
11. ___ inceptor
12. ___ interfector
13. ___ inventor
14. ___ lector
15. ___ līberātor
16. ___ monitor
17. ___ mōtor
18. ___ mūnītor
19. ___ rector
20. ___ reductor

a. reader
b. reminder or prompter
c. advisor or one who asks advice
d. shouter
e. giver
f. keeper, guardian
g. deliverer
h. teacher, instructor
i. murderer
j. restorer
k. mover or rocker
l. beginner
m. listener or pupil
n. receiver or approver
o. driver or charioteer
p. one who owes
q. protector, defender
r. discoverer
s. engineer
t. controller, governor

LESSON XLIX

CĪNEĀS ET PYRRHUS

 A **Ablative of respect/specification** The *ablative of respect* is also referred to in some books as the *ablative of specification*. It specifies assertions about distinctive qualities or circumstances.

Translate and compare.

1. Brūtus erat Caesaris amīcus.

_____

Nōmine sed nōn factīs amīcus erat.

_____

2. Firmī estis.

_____

Sententiīs vestrīs firmī estis.

_____

3. Is et ea sunt parēs.

_____

Annīs parēs sunt, sed neque dīligentiā neque fāmā.

_____

 B **Ablative of respect/specification** The following phrases illustrate the ablative of respect. Translate each, and then match each to the famous individual it describes.

    a. Alexander the Great
    b. Joan of Arc
    c. Napoleon Bonaparte
    d. George Patton
    e. George Washington

1. _____ prīmus bellō, prīmus pāce

_____

2. _____ corpore parvus sed magnus factīs bellī

_____

3. _____ dux Graecus etiam nunc fāmā ēgregius

_____

4. _____ nātūrā puella quae armīs et vestibus virī in Galliā

_____

_____

5. _____ dux quī omnēs numerō victōriārum in Secundō Bellō Terrārum superābat

_____

C **Latin syntax: case usage and verb tenses** Answer each question regarding the syntax of the passage on pages 332-333.

Identify the use of the ablative case illustrated by each of the following words.

1. castrīs   line 1   _____

2. celeritāte   line 4   _____

3. armīs   line 8   _____

4. celeritāte   line 12   _____

5. hostibus   line 14   _____

Identify the case of the following words, and state the reason for the use of that case.

6. lēgātus   line 1   _____

7. familiārī   line 3   _____

8. facile   line 8   _____

9. pācem   line 16   _____

10. mēcum   line 17   _____

Identify the tense of the following verbs from the passage.

11. monēbat   line 3   _____

12. erit   line 8   _____

13. respondit   line 11   _____

14. pellam   line 13   _____

15. faciēs   line 14   _____

THE ADVENTURES OF ULYSSES, ROMULUS, REMUS, AND PYRRHUS

UNIT IX REVIEW

 Roman architecture and engineering

As you have no doubt realized from the many photographs in your textbook, the Romans were remarkable engineers. Some of their building achievements are described in the following sentences. Using an encyclopedia entry on Roman architecture, provide answers to the following definitions. The letters you write in the highlighted boxes will spell a Latin noun of relevance to the subject.

1. Every day, three to four hundred million gallons of water were transported to Rome. Much of this was channeled to _____, huge buildings where the population exercised and socialized.

2. The Coliseum was a famous _____, in which men fought men, men fought animals, and animals fought animals.

3. The most popular public gathering place in ancient Rome was the _____, an oblong area where chariots raced.

4. The Romans developed and made wide use of this fundamental feature. It was a curved construction of brick or stone used to bear the weight of other masonry. It is known as the _____.

5. With many small pieces of colored glass or stone, the Romans composed a kind of decorative picture known as a/an _____.

6. This building material, made from bonded sand and gravel, was used by the Romans for road construction; it also figured prominently in buildings like the Pantheon: _____.

7. The most distinctive feature of the Pantheon is its hemispherical roof, also called a/an _____.

8. In Roman times, this building functioned as a court of law; it is now the name for a special kind of church. _____

9. Each civic center held at least one building in which sacrifices were offered; this center of religious activity was called a/an _____.

10. By using a series of curved structures to support the weight of material over an open space, the Romans created a/an _____, which is more commonly referred to as a tunnel.

11. In every Roman town there was a civic center, or _____.

12. The service through which water was brought to a Roman city was a/an _____.

1. ___ | ___ ___ ___ ___ ___

2. ___ ___ | ___ ___ ___ ___

3. ___ | ___ ___ ___

4. ___ ___ ___ | ___

5. ___ ___ ___ ___ | ___ ___ ___ ___ ___

6. ___ ___ ___ ___ ___ | ___ ___

7. ___ ___ | ___ ___

8. ___ ___ ___ ___ ___ | ___ ___ ___ ___

9. ___ | ___ ___ ___

10. ___ ___ ___ | ___ ___ ___

11. ___ ___ ___ | ___ ___ ___

12. ___ ___ | ___ ___ ___ ___ ___

B **Mottoes and phrases** See how many of the following mottoes and phrases you remember from earlier lessons. Although you are answering specific questions about each phrase, be prepared to translate each one aloud in class.

1. Vēnī, vīdī, vīcī.
   What do the verbs in this sentence have in common?

   _____

2. In hōc signō vincēs.
   What is the tense of the verb in this motto?

   _____

3. Fortūna *caeca* est.
   What is the case use of the italicized word?

   _____

4. Pāx vōbīscum.
   What use of the ablative case is illustrated by this phrase?

   _____

5. integer; miser
   What parts of speech are these cognates in Latin? In English?

   _____

6. data
   In English, should this word be modified with *this* or *these?*

   _____

7. in memoriam
   Which of the glossary's definitions for **in** best expresses its meaning in this phrase?

   _____

8. auxiliō ab altō
   Explain the usage (type) of each ablative noun.

   _____

9. Montānī semper līberī
   What verb is understood here?

   _____

10. paucī quōs aequus amat Iūppiter
    In this phrase, what does **aequus** modify?

    _____

11. *Deō* grātiās
    What is the case of the italicized word?

    _____

12. lēx scrīpta

12. lēx scrīpta

What form of the verb is **scrīpta?**

_____

13. mē iūdice

Of what construction is this phrase an example?

_____

14. P.S.

For what Latin word is this **S.** an abbreviation?

_____

15. ad fīn.

What is the case of the word for which **fīn.** is an abbreviation?

_____

UNIT X
MYTHS, LEGENDS, AND HISTORY OF EARLY GREECE AND ROME

LESSON L

SĀTURNUS ET IUPPITER

A **Review of pronouns** A pronoun, in Latin as well as in English, is a part of speech that takes the place of a noun. It therefore does not name, but refers to, a person, place, thing, or idea.

The pronouns you have already learned are grouped as personal pronouns, relative pronouns, and interrogative pronouns. Note the underlined words as you translate each sentence.

<u>Nōs</u> Gigantēs <u>quī</u> sumus filiī Terrae ōlim pugnāvimus pro rēgnum Olympī.

_____

<u>Quī quōs</u> in bellō *quōs* superāvērunt? (Double interrogative)

_____

B **Demonstratives** Demonstrative adjectives, often used as pronouns, form yet another group. Notice how the underlined Latin demonstratives are translated in the following sentences.

<u>Haec</u> est poena quam Iūppiter Gigantibus dedit.
This is the punishment which Jupiter gave to the Giants.

<u>Illī</u> ad Īnferōs missī sunt et semper in Tartarō tenēbuntur.
They (lit., those) were sent to the Underworld and will always be kept in Tartarus.

In Latin, these demonstratives are used far more often as pronouns than in English, because their inflected forms are more specific indicators of person, number, and gender. Note the underlined words as you translate:

Briareus nōn est captīvus in <u>hōc locō</u> quod <u>is</u> nōn cum reliquīs Gigantibus pugnāvit.

_____

_____

Officium <u>huius</u> est spectāre <u>illōs</u> Gigantēs quī malī erant.

_____

Remember that the personal pronouns **ego** and **tū** show no gender by themselves, although the gender of the noun to which they refer is usually clear from context. On the other hand, **quī, quis, hic,** and **ille** are fully declinable in all three genders. Note the respective differences in the nominative subjects of the following sentences.

Name _____ Date _____

Translate.

Ego sum discipulus. _____

Ego sum discipula. _____

Hic est discipulus. _____

Haec est discipula. _____

When referring to both genders, the masculine gender is used.

Hic et haec sunt discipulī. _____

Hī sunt discipulī. _____

C Give the corresponding plurals of each demonstrative.

1. hōc _____   6. illud _____

2. hoc _____   7. illum _____

3. huic _____   8. illa _____

4. hic _____   9. ille _____

5. hanc _____   10. illā _____

D **Agreement of demonstrative adjectives** For each of the following nouns, supply forms of
both demonstrative adjectives (**hic** and **ille**).

	HIC	ILLE
1. beneficia	_____ ;	_____
2. salūs	_____ ;	_____
3. lēge	_____ ;	_____
4. exemplīs	_____ ;	_____
5. cīvēs	_____ ;	_____
6. _or_	_____ ;	_____
7. mātrī	_____ ;	_____
8. poētae	_____ ;	_____
9. _or_	_____ ;	_____
10. _or_	_____ ;	_____

E **Demonstratives used as pronouns** Replace the underlined words in each sentence with corresponding forms of both **hic** and **ille**.

1. Dominus <u>servō</u> pecūniam dedit.

   _____   _____

2. Fēminae cum <u>virīs</u> labōrābant.

   _____   _____

3. <u>Ea</u> celeris est.

   _____   _____

4. Amīcī <u>rēgis</u> vēnerant.

   _____   _____

F **Special meanings of demonstratives** Translate the following sentences and answer questions 4 and 5.

1. Promēthēus et Epimētheus poenīs affectī sunt.

   _____

2. Ille ad saxum ligātus est et ab aquilā petītus est.

   _____

3. Hic Pandoram in mātrimōnium dūxit et ab eā multa mala accēpit.

   _____

4. Which brother was enchained and attacked?

   _____

5. Which brother suffered because of his wife?

   _____

LESSON LI

CAEDICIUS FORTIS

 Ablative of time when/within which The *ablative of time when* and *time within which,* like the ablatives of means, respect, and (sometimes) manner, do not use a preposition in Latin. The ablative of time is easy to recognize, for it always occurs with expressions having to do with time. The following list, in fact, anticipating a few entries from future vocabularies, is a fairly complete one for these two ablatives of time.

unā hōrā	*in one hour, within one hour*
hōrā prīmā	*at the first hour, in the first hour*

Notice that the Latin preposition **in** is not used with expressions of time. It is only used when physical locations are intended.

		ABLATIVE FORMS	
		SINGULAR	PLURAL
hōra, hōrae, f.	*hour*	hōrā	hōrīs
annus, annī, m.	*year*	annō	annīs
aestās, aestātis, f.	*summer*	aestāte	aestātibus
hiems, hiemis, f.	*winter*	hieme	hiemibus
autumnus, autumnī, m.	*fall*	autumnō	autumnīs
vēr, vēris, n.	*spring*	vēre	vēribus
tempus, temporis, n.	*time*	tempore	temporibus
nox, noctis, f.	*night*	nocte	noctibus
diēs, diēī, m.	*day*	diē	diēbus
vigilia, vigiliae, f.	*watch*	vigiliā	vigiliīs

For questions 1 through 4 below, answer in Latin, using the correct case and number and the *ablative of time when* construction. Select from the list of vocabulary given above.

1. In what season are you most likely to see a cornucopia as the centerpiece of a large family dinner?

_____

2. In what season do we celebrate the passing of the old year?

_____

3. In what season do migrating birds fly north again?

_____

4. In what season do we celebrate our nation's Independence Day?

_____

5. (Within a few hours), you can travel by car from Rome to Brindisi.

_____

6. (In ancient times*), the journey took much longer.

_____

*antiquus, -a, -um: old, ancient

7. (In the year 37 B.C)., Vergil and Horace made this trip with the Emperor Augustus.

_____

8. (By day), they traveled on foot and in carriages.

_____

9. (At night), they stayed with friends or took rooms at an inn.

_____

10. (In the watches of the night), these wary travelers posted slaves as a guard against highwaymen.

_____

LESSON LII

CĪVITĀS RŌMĀNA

 Demonstrative *is, ea, id* A third demonstrative pronoun is introduced in this lesson. It should look familiar to you already. Like **hic** and **ille,** it can be used as either a pronoun or an adjective. As a demonstrative adjective, singular forms of **is** will be variously translated as either *this* or *that.* In the plural, forms of this adjective will be translated as either *these* or *those.*

Bear in mind that **is** does not focus as precisely as **hic** and **ille** do. As an adjective, **is** is used almost the same way the definite article *the* is used in English.

Latin, of course, does not use the definite article. **Is,** on the other hand, is very common. It is perhaps the very frequency of its use that accounts for the occasional need to translate as *the.*

Rewrite the following phrases, replacing the demonstrative adjective with corresponding forms of **is.** Then translate each phrase.

1. hanc partem _____   _____

2. illō tempore _____   _____

3. hī hostēs _____   _____

4. illīus cīvitātis _____   _____

5. haec corpora _____   _____

Whenever they function as *pronouns* (i.e., not as adjectives), forms of **is, ea, id** are best translated with English third person pronouns: he, she, it, they, etc.

EXEMPLĪ GRĀTIĀ

Senātōrēs Rōmānōs monuērunt.	*The senators warned the Romans.*
Senātōres eōs monuērunt.	*The senators warned them.*
Eī eōs monuērunt.	*They warned them.*

The genitive forms of these Latin pronouns are particularly important: **eius** can mean *his, her(s),* or *its,* while **eōrum, eārum,** and **eōrum** mean *their(s).* English possessive pronouns *her, his,* and *its* are gender-specific only in the singular; Latin **eōrum** and **eārum** only in the plural.

LATIN FOR AMERICANS, LEVEL 1
UNIT X LESSON LII
WORKBOOK

B **Case identification** Match the following:

1. _____ eum a. masculine accusative singular
2. _____ eīs b. feminine accusative singular
3. _____ eās c. masculine and neuter ablative singular
4. _____ eōrum d. feminine ablative singular
5. _____ eam e. feminine nominative plural
6. _____ eō f. masculine and neuter genitive plural
7. _____ eōs g. feminine genitive plural
8. _____ eārum h. all genders: dative and ablative plural
9. _____ eā i. masculine accusative plural
10. _____ eae j. feminine accusative plural

C *Is* **as a demonstrative adjective** Replace the forms of **is** with corresponding forms of both **hic** and **ille** and then translate the original sentence.

1. Prīmō annō reī pūblicae [509 B.C.], Brūtus populum dūxit; Rōmānī <u>eum</u> et Collātīnum cōnsulēs fēcērunt.

_____   _____

_____   _____

2. <u>Eō</u> tempore, Rōmānī rēgēs pepulerant.

_____   _____

3. Tamen fīliī <u>eius</u> cōnsilia cum hostibus cīvitātis Rōmānae cēpērunt.

_____   _____

_____   _____

4. <u>Ea</u> cōnsilia patrī <u>eōrum</u> nūntiāta sunt.

_____   _____

_____   _____

_____   _____

5. Quod erat vir ēgregius virtūte, Brūtus, pater miser, <u>eōs</u> fīliōs interfēcit.

_____   _____

_____   _____

D **Pronouns** Identify the gender, case, and number of each of the following pronoun by circling all the descriptive terms that apply to each of them.

1. nōbīs   \<masc> \<fem> \<neut> \<nom> \<gen> \<dat> \<acc> \<abl> \<sing> \<pl>

2. cuius   \<masc> \<fem> \<neut> \<nom> \<gen> \<dat> \<acc> \<abl> \<sing> \<pl>

3. illī   \<masc> \<fem> \<neut> \<nom> \<gen> \<dat> \<acc> \<abl> \<sing> \<pl>

4. hārum   \<masc> \<fem> \<neut> \<nom> \<gen> \<dat> \<acc> \<abl> \<sing> \<pl>

5. quid   \<masc> \<fem> \<neut> \<nom> \<gen> \<dat> \<acc> \<abl> \<sing> \<pl>

6. is   \<masc> \<fem> \<neut> \<nom> \<gen> \<dat> \<acc> \<abl> \<sing> \<pl>

7. eīs   \<masc> \<fem> \<neut> \<nom> \<gen> \<dat> \<acc> \<abl> \<sing> \<pl>

8. id   \<masc> \<fem> \<neut> \<nom> \<gen> \<dat> \<acc> \<abl> \<sing> \<pl>

9. eius   \<masc> \<fem> \<neut> \<nom> \<gen> \<dat> \<acc> \<abl> \<sing> \<pl>

10. ea   \<masc> \<fem> \<neut> \<nom> \<gen> \<dat> \<acc> \<abl> \<sing> \<pl>

Name _____ Date _____

LESSON LIII

MIDĀS

 Demonstrative *īdem, eadem, idem* Until now, all inflected Latin nouns and pronouns have followed one general rule: their case endings have been shown by their final syllable(s). However, certain pronouns do not follow this pattern. Instead, they are declined with a common suffix, which is *preceded* by a case ending.

In the current lesson, you are introduced to one such demonstrative **īdem.** Notice its similarity to **is.** Many of its forms, in fact, actually contain the corresponding form of **is** followed by the suffix **-dem.**

Replace the italicized words in the following sentences with a corresponding form of **īdem,** then translate the new sentence. The word replaced may be either a noun, pronoun, or adjective.

1. *Multa* vīdī. _____

2. *Is* et *ea* sunt amīcī. _____

3. *Puerō* praemium dedimus. _____

4. *Verbīs* hominēs incitāvit. _____

5. Exemplum *illōrum* nōn erat clārum. _____

Give a form of **īdem** that agrees with each word or phrase.

6. tempore _____

7. lībertātis _____

8. nāvēs longae _____

9. factum _____

10. prīmos rēgēs _____

 Demonstrative *īdem* Translate the following sentences to get an idea of the contexts in which you will encounter **īdem.**

1. Cicerō pueritiam* in oppidō Arpīno** ēgit.

_____

***pueritia, -ae,** f. *boyhood (years)*
****Arpīnum, -ī,** n. *Arpinum, a town in Latium*

2. Marius, dux ēgregius, in <u>eōdem</u> locō habitāverat.

_____

3. Annō 53 B.C. triumvir* Crassus in Parthiā interfectus est.

_____

***triumvir, -ī,** m. *triumvir, member of three person government*

4. <u>Eōdem</u> tempore Caesar in Galliā pugnābat.

_____

5. Sacra Via et Via Flāminia nōtae viae in Rōmā antīquā erant.

_____

6. Etiam nunc in Italiā <u>eaedam</u> viae vidērī possunt.

_____

7. Senatōrēs Rōmānī Octāviānō nōmen "Imperātor*" dedērunt.

_____

*imperātor, -ōris, m. *commander (in chief), emperor*

8. <u>Eīdem</u> senatōrēs <u>eīdem</u> hominī nōmen "Augustus" dedērunt.

_____

9. Caesar in Hispāniā Galliāque pugnāvit.

_____

10. Imperātor Hadriānus iter ad <u>eāsdem</u> prōvinciās fēcit.

_____

LESSON LIV

HORĀTIUS

 Demonstrative pronoun/adjective *ipse, ipsa, ipsum* Yet another type of demonstrative pronoun/adjective is the intensive **ipse.** Pay careful attention to the different use of pronouns ending in *-self* and *-selves* in English. Some are intensive, and others are reflexive.

> Pompey <u>himself</u> led the troops. (intensive)

> He considered <u>himself</u> Rome's greatest general. (reflexive)

The intensive in Latin is **ipse.** It is never used reflexively, i.e. to show action reflected back on a subject. Its purpose is *merely to add emphasis.* It agrees in Latin with the word(s) it describes in gender, number, and case.

Circle the English pronouns that are used intensively in the following sentences. Disregard those that are used reflexively.

1. Because of his victories on Sicily, Pompey was first called "Magnus" by Sulla himself.

2. This young knight said to Sulla: "Despite my age, I want a triumph for myself."

3. He later rallied to the needs of Rome when the senate declared, "We Romans must defend ourselves against pirates."

4. The pirates themselves were not only defeated but also resettled by Pompey.

5. Caesar and Crassus allied themselves to this up-and-coming military figure.

 Intensive vs. reflexive Remember that the intensive **idem** is not essential to the structure of the sentence; i.e., a sentence containing an intensive can still be understood if it is omitted. If, on the other hand, you omit a reflexive pronoun, a direct or indirect object of a verb is often lost. Consider the following.

> The women defended themselves.

You cannot omit the reflexive pronoun above without losing the direct object.

Indicate whether the underlined words in the following sentences are intensive or reflexive, and then translate the intensive words with a form of **ipse.**

1. I myself saw the man.   \<intensive\>   \<reflexive\> _____

2. I saw myself in the mirror.   \<intensive\>   \<reflexive\> _____

3. The host prepared the meal himself.   \<intensive\>   \<reflexive\> _____

4. The host prepared himself.   \<intensive\>   \<reflexive\> _____

MYTHS, LEGENDS, AND HISTORY OF EARLY GREECE AND ROME

UNIT X REVIEW

A **Derivatives** Circle the best answer based on your knowledge of Latin root words.

1. Which of the following is *tangible?*

   a. death   **b.** summer   **c.** power   **d.** dew

2. Which of the following is a *sedentary* job?

   a. typist   **b.** hairdresser   **c.** server   **d.** letter carrier

3. Which of the following words does not derive from **colō?**

   a. agriculture   **b.** semicolon   **c.** colonist   **d.** cult

4. Which of the following words is a synonym for *aspire?*

   a. die   **b.** lapse   **c.** hope   **d.** influence

5. Which of the following circumstances may be *intimidating?*

   a. a pop quiz   **c.** a chirping cricket

   b. watching a sports game   **d.** taking a day off

6. How might your math teacher handle an *infraction?*

   a. put it on the chalkboard   **c.** call the school nurse

   b. assign a detention   **d.** take a sick day

7. What does the Spanish word *esperanza* mean?

   a. prophecy   **b.** awakening   **c.** experience   **d.** hope

8. When do *concurrent* events take place?

   a. one after the other   **c.** at the same time

   b. very quickly   **d.** in adjacent areas

9. If your illness is in *remission,* what have happened to its symptoms?

   a. come back   **c.** let up

   b. gotten worse   **d.** greatly improved

Name _____ Date _____

10. Which of the following words does not derive from **ūnus?**

    a. unitary   b. uniform   c. unimpaired   d. unicorn

11. The Latin word **genus** is most likely to appear on a vocabulary list for which discipline?

    a. driver ed   b. sociology   c. physics   d. biology

12. What is a good antonym for *cordiality?*

    a. rudeness   b. apprehension   c. intelligence   d. individuality

13. What can the word *precipitous* be used to describe?

    a. a kidnapping   b. a cliff face   c. a treasure   d. individuality

14. What are you doing if you are *aestivating* on the Riviera?

    a. getting arrested   c. residing permanently

    b. spending the summer there   d. getting lost

15. A *nihilist* believes in the value of what?

    a. nothing at all   c. new ideas

    b. capital punishment   d. economic sanctions

ROMAN GODS AND ROMAN HEROES

LESSON LVI

CICERŌ ET TĪRŌ

 Pronominal adjectives The adjectives in this lesson are often called irregular. However, they differ from other adjectives in the singular forms of only two cases—the genitive and the dative. Note that the "irregular" genitive and dative singulars of these adjectives have the same endings as other pronominal adjectives and pronouns that you have studied. The other twenty-four forms of these adjectives follow the first and second declensions.

EXEMPLĪ GRĀTIĀ

GENITIVE SINGULAR	DATIVE SINGULAR
cuius	cui
huius	huic
illīus	illī
eius	eī
ipsīus	ipsī
alterius	alterī

Since you have grown accustomed to translating such phrases as **nōmen huius librī** or **fīnitimus eī agrō,** you will not find it any harder to use these similarly inflected adjectives.

To remember them as a group, you may use the following mnemonic device: the first letters of these adjectives, as listed below, spell the Latin words **ūnus nauta.**

Ūnus, *one*

Nūllūs, *none*

Ūllus, *any*

Sōlus, *only*

Neuter, *neither* (of two)

Alter, *the other* (of two)

Uter[que], *which* (of two)/*each* (of two)

Tōtus, *entire*

Alius, *another*

Name _____ Date _____

Translate each phrase paying careful attention to case endings. The dative with adjective construction introduced in Lesson LXIII is commonly used here.

1. nūllī secundus _____

2. amīcus neutrī virō _____

3. sacer tōtī patriae _____

4. nōtus sōlī mihi _____

5. aestās utrīus annī _____

6. pretium unīus casae _____

7. locus alīus proelī _____

8. arma alterius mīlitis _____

9. pars ūllīus cōnsilī _____

10. fīnitimus utrīque terminō _____

B **Pronouns/pronominal adjectives** Choose the correct answer:

1. Which of the following cannot be masculine?
   a. huic   **b.** eīdem   **c.** quid   **d.** eius

2. Which of the following pronouns is both singular and plural?
   a. meī   **b.** cui   **c.** tuī   **d.** quae

3. Which of the following cannot be dative?
   a. illīs   **b.** eī   **c.** quī   **d.** hīs

4. Which of the following is neuter and accusative?
   a. hic   **b.** hōc   **c.** hāc   **d.** hoc

5. Which of the following is not both an adjective and a pronoun?
   a. quī   **b.** quibus   **c.** quae   **d.** quid

6. Which of the following is feminine?
   a. eum   **b.** hunc   **c.** eōrundem   **d.** quō

7. Which of the following cannot be singular?
   a. mihi   **b.** ea   **c.** nōbīs   **d.** ipsa

8. Which of the following is a demonstrative adjective?
   a. illa   **b.** vōbīs   **c.** nūlla   **d.** quā

9. Which of the following must be only one case?
   a. ūllī   **b.** īdem   **c.** illī   **d.** ipsī

10. Which of the following is plural?

    a. ipsīus   **b.** huic   **c.** īdem   **d.** quae

11. Which of the following is not genitive?

    a. vestrum   **b.** quōrum   **c.** tuī   **d.** eandem

12. Which of the following is masculine?

    a. haec   **b.** illud   **c.** īdem   **d.** ipsa

13. Which of the following means entire?

    a. tōta   **b.** omne   **c.** quī   **d.** sōlus

14. Which of the following can mean myself?

    a. ea   **b.** ipse   **c.** idem   **d.** ille

15. Which of the following can mean his, her, or its?

    a. eiusdem   **b.** is   **c.** eīus   **d.** eōrum

LESSON LVII

QUĪNTUS CICERŌ ET POMPŌNIA

 Present participles In this lesson, you are introduced to present participles. Answer the following.

1. A participle is a form of a verb that can be used to modify which two parts of speech?

_____   _____

The fourth principal part of verbs given in your textbook as you recall, is often a *perfect passive participle*. Because these participles derive from verbs, these modifiers have tense and voice.

2. Identify the tense and voice of **oppressus** (the fourth principal part of **opprimō**).

_____

There are additional participles of **opprimō** in the present and future tenses. First let's look at the present participle. Here is a present participle with its meaning:

opprimēns, opprimentis   *oppressing*

Translate these nominatives.

3. nūntius accēdēns _____

4. nāvis accēdēns _____

5. bellum accēdēns _____

Note that one form (**accēdēns**) is used for all three genders in the nominative singular.

Like all other present participles, **accēdēns** also has one genitive singular:

accēden __ __ __.

Notice the predictable change of the consonants **ns** to __ __ in the base. Because it is a verbal *adjective,* and because the base ends in a double consonant, the participle's declension must be what type?

_____.

Which of the following Latin words would be translated as *-ing* words in English? Place an X by each present participle.

6. _____ trāns   **11.** _____ contentum

7. _____ agēns   **12.** _____ stantem

8. _____ impedientī   **13.** _____ montem

9. _____ nūntī   **14.** _____ sententiīs

10. _____ frūmentum   **15.** _____ ventīs

B **Present participles: four conjugations** Create and translate the nominative singular forms of the present participles for each verb.

	PARTICIPLE	MEANING
1. pugnō	_____	_____
2. sedeō	_____	_____
3. tangō	_____	_____
4. recipiō	_____	_____
5. expediō	_____	_____

C **Derivatives from present participles** Using the bases from the genitive singulars of the five participles that you have listed above, create the following derivatives.

1. re _ _ _ _ _ _ _ _   (fighting back)

2. _ _ _ _ _ _ _ _ ary   (sitting down)

3. _ _ _ _ _ _ _ _ ial   (touching upon)

4. _ _ _ _ _ _ _ _ _ _   (a person receiving something)

5. _ _ _ _ _ _ _ _ _ _   (something useful for bringing about a desired result)

D **Agreement of present participles** Choose the noun from each group that agrees in case, number, and gender with each participle.

1. dubitāns

    a. populum   **b.** vōs   **c.** ego   **d.** paucī

2. dubitantis

    a. fīnitimīs   **b.** magistrae   **c.** fīliābus   **d.** patrī

3. dubitantī

    a. amīcī   **b.** puella   **c.** captīve   **d.** servō

4. dubitantem

    a. ducum   **b.** poētārum   c. fīliām   **d.** nostrum

5. dubitante

    a. vōce   **b.** ordō   **c.** socī   **d.** meī

6. dubitantēs

    a. mīles   **b.** barbarī   **c.** memoriā   **d.** civitās

7. dubitantia

    a. agricola   **b.** dea   **c.** rēgīna   **d.** corda

8. dubitantium

    a. equōrum   **b.** nūntium   **c.** dominum   **d.** sorōrem

9. dubitantibus

    a. nauta   **b.** colōnus   **c.** cīvis   **d.** virīs

10. dubitantēs

    a. discipulōs   **b.** hominī   **c.** inimīcīs   **d.** signa

 Future active participle Some verbs that you have learned (e.g., **sum, esse, fuī, futūrus**) have future active participles as their fourth principal parts.

You have already memorized many future participles, which you can now use. Provide and translate each fourth principal part, following the model.

    oppressūrus, -a, -um   *going to oppress*

        FOURTH PRINCIPAL PART   TRANSLATION

1. absum   _____   _____

2. adsum   _____   _____

3. antecēdō   _____   _____

4. contendō   _____   _____

5. currō   _____   _____

6. discēdō   _____   _____

7. prōcēdō   _____   _____

8. remaneō   _____   _____

9. sedeō   _____   _____

10. stō   _____   _____

 Present and future participle compared Both of the participles introduced in this lesson are active. Unlike the perfect passive participle, both of these participles, present and future, will sometimes have objects. Study the following sentences.

In hōc pictūrā vir animalia agēns Hannibal est.

Elephantōs cibum armaque portantēs trāns Alpēs trādūxit.

1. What is/are the objects(s) of **agēns** in the first sentence?

_____

2. What is/are the objects(s) of **portantēs** in the second sentence?

_____

The participle word modified by the participle, and its object(s) in both sentences constitute what is called a *participial phrase.*

Examine the following sentence:

Currit
(S)he runs.
(S)he is running.

One would never write **est currēns** to express the thought *(s)he is running;* **currit** (present tense) is sufficient.

Notice that, with the future tense, **curret** means *she* or *he will run,* but **cursūrus est** can only mean *he is going to run.* Why can't this future participle combination with **est** mean *she is going to run?*

Future active participles, like all participles, are sometimes best translated as relative clauses:

Hannibal proelium cum Rōmānīs commissūrus dē montibus in Italiam vēnit.

Hannibal, about to begin battle, . . .
Hannibal, who was going to begin battle, . . .

In the preceding sentence, **proelium... commissūrus** is the participial phrase.

LESSON LVIII

CINCINNĀTUS

A **Vocabulary** Answer based on your knowledge of Latin vocabulary.

1. Computers use a blinking light called a *cursor*. What does that mean, literally?

   _____

2. What does a movie *projector,* by definition, do to film images?

   _____

3. What is a person who *safeguards* objects in a museum for display often called?

   _____

4. A *dictator* in ancient Rome was a man who was given absolute power to do what for a six-month period?

   _____

5. What Latin word provides the root for the geographical term *equator?*

   _____

B **Perfect active infinitive** As you can see, you are expanding your knowledge of verbs in this unit. Infinitives have tense and voice.

1. What is the tense of **ostendere?** _____

2. What is the voice of **dīcere?** _____

3. What is the tense of **esse?** _____

4. What is the voice of **prohibērī?** _____

Verbs also have perfect active infinitives. These forms, which are based on the perfect stem, are translated with the English auxiliary *have.*

> **cōnstitisse**   *to have stopped*
> **dīxisse**   *to have said*

Create and translate similar infinitives for each of the following verbs.

	PERFECT ACTIVE	
	INFINITIVES	TRANSLATIONS
5. superō	_____	_____
6. augeō	_____	_____
7. claudō	_____	_____
8. interficiō	_____	_____
9. audiō	_____	_____

These infinitives can be used like those you have already learned, i.e., as subjects . . .

> **Ēgisse vītam tuam inter hominēs in concordiā bonum est.**
> *To have spent your life in harmony among people is a good (thing).*

or as objects....

> **Nōnne cupis vītam tuam bene ēgisse?**
> *Don't you want to have lived your life well?*

C **Review of infinitives** Translate.

1. iacere _____

2. spērāvisse _____

3. pellī _____

4. tendere _____

5. potuisse _____

6. tangī _____

Translate.

7. to be present* _____

8. to have sought _____

9. to have been well* _____
    *Note that this is not passive, even though it seems to be.

10. to be loved _____

LESSON LIX

BELLA

 Vocabulary In the vocabulary for this lesson, you are introduced to several words with interesting uses. One such word is the conjunction **sī**. An English translation of a subordinate clause introduced by **sī** will often omit the helping verb *will* that typically indicates the future tense.

EXEMPLĪ GRĀTIĀ

> **Sī cūrā magnā spectābis, id vidēbis.**
> *If you (will) watch very carefully, you will see it.*

Mūnus *(public service)* also refers to a *gladiatorial show*. A **lūdus** is a *play* or *game*. **Lūdī circensēs** were "racetrack" games, i.e., chariot races. Which was more popular with the Romans? How do the relative sizes of the Coliseum and Circus Maximus indicate this preference?

_____

_____

Solvō is often used in the idiomatic expression **nāvem solvere.** As an idiom, this phrase means to *launch a ship.* How do you explain the connection between the literal (word for word) meaning and the idiomatic meaning?

_____

Notice that **ācer,** like **celer,** has three nominative singular endings. Give nominative forms of the following.

1. a sharp manner _____

2. a sharp punishment _____

3. a sharp word _____

Now that you know the word **urbs** *(city),* you will want to reserve the word **oppidum** for true towns. Rome and Carthage, for instance, were not really **oppida.** They were **urbēs.** A *village* was called a **vīcus,** from which we derive the English word *vicinity.* A *fort* was a **castellum** and, in a sense, was also a *community.*

 Perfect passive and future active infinitive The two infinitives introduced in this lesson are based on participles that you have already learned. The tense and voice of these participles are the same as the tense and voice of the infinitives that build on them.

1. What is the perfect passive participle of **solvō?**

_____

2. How is this participle translated?

3. What is the perfect passive infinitive of **solvō?**

_____

4. How is this infinitive translated?

_____

5. What is the future active participle of **removeō?**

_____

6. How is this participle translated?

_____

7. What is the future active infinitive of **removeō?**

_____

8. How is this infinitive translated?

_____

Remember that the perfect active infinitive uses the perfect stem rather than the participial stem and is just one word.

9. Using the Latin verb **ostendō,** how do you *say to have shown?*

_____

10. With the same verb, how do you say *to have been shown?*

_____

There are five infinitives for transitive verbs. A table illustrating all five is given below. Translate the infinitives shown in the table, and reproduce the chart in full with the verb **prohibeō**.

	ACTIVE	TRANSLATION	PASSIVE	TRANSLATION
PRESENT	iacere	_____	iacī	_____
PERFECT	iēcisse	_____	iactus esse	_____
FUTURE	iactūrus esse	_____		

Nota•Bene The future passive infinitive is a rarely encountered form that you may learn in upper-level Latin studies.

	ACTIVE	TRANSLATION	PASSIVE	TRANSLATION
PRESENT	_____	to prevent	_____	to be prevented
PERFECT	_____	to have prevented	_____	to have been prevented
			_____	
FUTURE	_____	to be going to (about to) prevent		

Name _____ Date _____

C Infinitives and participles Match each form with its meaning.

1. _____ sciēns   a. to be going to know
2. _____ scīre   b. to be known
3. _____ scīrī   c. knowing
4. _____ scītus   d. (having been) known
5. _____ scīvisse   e. to have known
6. _____ scītus esse   f. to know
7. _____ scītūrus   g. going to know
8. _____ scītūrus esse   h. to have been known

Use the stem of **scīo**'s present participle to complete the following sentence.

9. If you know things before they happen, you might be called

   pre _____.

D Practice with participles and infinitives Translate each with precise observance of tense and voice.

1. putāns _____
2. putātus _____
3. putātūrus _____
4. putāre _____
5. putārī _____
6. putāvisse _____
7. putātus esse _____
8. putātūrus esse _____

Answer the following based on your knowledge of the verb **putō**.

9. Based on the meanings of the following English words, which does not derive from **putō**?

   a. compute   **b.** disputable   **c.** input   **d.** reputation

10. An officer of the law who is appointed to act in the place of, or think for, a higher official is called a _____.

Name _____ Date _____

 Indirect statement construction The newly introduced infinitives appear, for the most part, in sentences that contain *indirect statements.* Sentences of this kind, also referred to as *indirect discourse,* are introduced by a particular class of verbs. The following is a partial list of these verbs.

CONJUGATION	1	2	3	4
	clāmō	doceō	(cog)nōscō	audiō
	nūntiō	respondeō	dīcō	sciō
	putō	videō	ostendō	sentiō
	spērō		scrībō	
			crēdō*	
			intellegō*	

*These verbs will be introduced in future units, but are just as easily learned now in this context.

Notice that these verbs comprise a list of functions that include *thought processes, verbal expressions,* and *all five senses.*

Indirect statements are *noun clauses* used as the direct objects of the "head words" listed above. Head words comprise verbs meaning *say, think, believe, hear,* etc.—any verb having its origin from a person's head.

As clauses, indirect statements must have subjects and verbs. The verbs of these clauses, however, are *infinitives,* and their subjects are expressed in the *accusative* case. English often uses the word *that* as an introduction to such a clause. Latin uses no such introductory word.

Which of the English verbs listed below could introduce the following indirect statement? Circle all correct responses.

1. I am paying . . .

2. I hope . . .

3. I am working . . .   **virum adesse.**

4. I understand . . .

5. I am reporting . . .

Translate each indirect statement.

6. Audiō carrōs accēdere.

_____

7. Cognōscit hostēs superārī.

_____

8. Sciuntne sociōs fīnitimōs esse?

_____

9. Dīcitne nūntius virōs valēre?

_____

10. Putātisne Americam hodiernam* ā Rōmānīs antīquīs addūcī?

_____

*modern

LATIN FOR AMERICANS, LEVEL 1
UNIT XI   LESSON LIX
WORKBOOK

LESSON LX

CORIOLĀNUS

 A **Indirect statement concepts** Answer based on your reading.

1. What relationship determines the tense of an indicative verb?

   _____

2. What relationship determines the tense of an infinitive?

   _____

Carefully study the following.

   Most Latin students <u>realize</u> that they <u>learn</u> a large amount of English in their Latin classes.

   You probably <u>realized</u> long ago that you <u>were learning</u> English in your Latin class.

3. What are the indicative verbs in the preceding sentences? And what tenses are they?

   _____

4. To express these sentences in Latin, infinitives are required. What tenses should those infinitives be?

   _____

Compare the two preceding sentences to the following two pairs.

   Your Latin teacher <u>hopes</u> that you <u>will remember</u> much of what you studied.

   When you took your last big English exam, he or she hoped that you <u>would remember</u> to look for Latin roots in the vocabulary section.

   Scores on college entrance exams typically show that Latin students <u>have acquired</u> an excellent English vocabulary.

   In a recent analysis of these scores, educators <u>showed</u> that Latin students <u>had acquired</u> a substantial advantage for college studies.

Analyze the preceding examples and tell which verbs would be translated in Latin with an infinitive and the tense that would be used.

5. _____

6. _____

7. _____

8. _____

Name _____ Date _____

 B Direct and indirect statement Translate the following five direct thoughts or statements and place them in the appropriate balloons in the illustration. Then translate the indirect statements regarding the following situations.

1. Hic est magnus!

_____

2. Certē haec victōria facilis erit.

_____

3. Diūtius* dubitāvistis!

*too long

4. Pignus* meum āmittētur.

*wager

5. Prō hīs mūneribus pecūnia mea bene ācta est.

_____

Now translate the following indirect statements about the preceding illustration.

6. Videt alterum gladiātōrem magnum esse.

_____

7. Sentit victōriam facilem futūram esse.

_____

8. Clāmat gladiātōrēs diūtius dubitāre.

_____

9. Putat pignus suum* malum fuisse.

_____

10. Dīcit pecūniam suam* prō hīs mūneribus bene actam esse.

_____

*his

Indirect statement translation Practice translating indirect statements in the following sentences. Be sure to consider carefully the tense and voice of the infinitive and its relation to the "head" verb first.

1. Putō reliquōs adfutūrōs esse.

_____

2. Respondērunt nautās nāvēs nōn solūtūrōs esse.

_____

3. Crēdēbāmus sociōs salūtem invēnisse.

_____

4. Vidēbitis nihil āmissum esse.

_____

5. Ostendunt signa ā hostibus capta recipī.

_____

6. Numquam intellegēmus aliōs nōn linguam Latīnam amāre.

_____

7. Illō tempore spērābam amīcum meum revertūrum esse.

_____

8. Dux nūntiāvit mīlitēs Rōmānōs bene pugnāvisse.

_____

9. Num audīverat omnia ad eōs quī exspectant venīre?

_____

10. Nōnne cognōvistī tempus fugere?

_____

D **Indirect statement: Quis sum?** Carefully translate each sentence. Then match each to the individual who said it.

    a. John Paul Jones
    b. Abraham Lincoln
    c. Oliver Hazard Perry
    d. Will Rogers
    e. George Washington

1. _____ Sociīs dīxī mē nōndum* pugnāre incēpisse.
   *not yet

_____

2. _____ Scrīpsī mē numquam hominem quem nōn amāvī invēnisse.

_____

3. _____ Populō Americānō nūntiāvī nōs hostēs invēnisse et eōs nostrōs esse.

_____

_____

4. _____ Nōvī nātiōnem semiservilem* et semilīberam nōn dūrāre* posse.
   *Semi- *half;* Servīlis *servile.*
   *endure

_____

5. _____ Patrī meō respondī mē nōn falsum dīcere posse.

_____

Name _____ Date _____

ROMAN GODS AND ROMAN HEROES

UNIT XI
REVIEW

 Practice with participles: Roman art Our knowledge of Roman customs is based not only on written accounts that have survived to the present day but also on details of daily life that are illustrated in ancient works of art. You may wish to refer to the page numbers of your textbook where some of the artworks are reproduced.

Translate each sentence.

1. In operibus musaeīs* et in sculptūrīs** vītam Rōmānōrum laborantium vidēre possumus (page 389).

   _____

   _____

   *opus musaeum: *mosaic work*
   **sculptūra: *sculpture (both free-standing statues and reliefs)*

2. In ūnō locō pastōrem spectantem ovēs* vidēmus (page 411), in aliō, Vestālēs Virginēs colentēs deam, in tertiō locō, aurigās** agentēs equōs in Circō.

   _____

   _____

   *ovēs: *sheep*
   **aurigās: *chariot drivers*

3. In pāginā CCLXXI librī tuī est statua clārī Rōmānī facientis verba in Forō.

   _____

   _____

4. In multīs sculptūrīs virī puerīque lūdentēs ostenduntur (page 306).

   _____

   _____

5. Inter sculptūrās in Columnā Trāiānā, vidēmus mīlitēs castra ponentēs et proelia incipientēs (page 114).

   _____

   _____

6. Ūnus sculptor antīquus virōs clārōs līberīs cibum dōnantēs repraesentāvit.

   _____

   _____

7. In Arā* Pācis imāginēs civium vestēs fōrmālēs gerentium et sacra pūblica gerentium
cōnservātae sunt.

_____

_____

* **Arā,** *altar*

8. Ab sculptūrīs antīquīs, paene spīrantibus aut mōtūris, multa dē vītā Rōmānā nōscere possumus.

_____

_____

UNIT XII
CLASSICAL MYTHS AND PORTRAITS OF ROMAN HEROES

LESSON LXI

QUATTUOR AETĀTĒS

 A Comparison of Adjectives Most adjectives you have learned so far assign qualities to the words that they modify.

EXEMPLĪ GRĀTIĀ

firma amīcitia	*firm friendship*
inimīcus rēx	*unfriendly king*
supplicium grave	*serious punishment*

However, things can possess differing *degrees* of a given quality. Some friendships are *firmer* than others. Some punishments are *very* severe. In Latin, these *differences of degree* are expressed by spelling changes.

For most adjectives, the letters **-ior** (masculine and feminine) and **-ius** (neuter) are added to its base to make the adjective *comparative*. Except for the neuter nominative (and accusative) **-ius,** all case forms add third declension endings to this sign.

For the superlative adjectives, the sign **-issm-** is needed, giving the endings **-issimus, -issima, -issimum** (first and second declensions) for the nominative forms. Superlatives are declined as first/second declension adjectives.

EXEMPLĪ GRĀTIĀ

firmio, firmius	*more firm, firmer, too firm, rather firm*
firmissimus, firmissima, firmissimum	*most firm, firmest, very firm*

Supply a form of each English noun that agrees with the given adjective. Then translate each adjective.

		LATIN NOUN	TRANSLATION
1. longiōrēs	roads *(acc.)*	_____	_____
2. latiōrem	field *(acc.)*	_____	_____
3. certissima	authority *(nom.)*	_____	_____
4. timidiōrēs	boys *(nom.)*	_____	_____
5. parātissimī	soldiers *(nom.)*	_____	_____
6. familiāris	land *(gen.)*	_____	_____
7. tardissimō	labor *(abl.)*	_____	_____
8. pauciōra	towns *(nom.)*	_____	_____
9. firmiōrī	protection *(dat.)*	_____	_____
10. commūne	duty *(nom.)*	_____	_____

B **Comparative adjectives** Remember that positive adjectives of the third declension are *i*-stem, while all *comparative* adjectives belong to the third declension. Change each adjective to the comparative degree and then translate.

1. in familiārī locō _____

_____

2. nōbilia facta *(nom. or acc.)* _____

_____

3. ūtilium verbōrum _____

_____

4. famous author *(abl.)* _____

_____

5. calm seas *(acc. pl.)* _____

_____

C **Comparative** Often, when the comparative degree is used, a reference is made to another person or thing that is the basis for the comparison.

    Helen of Sparta was lovelier <u>than all other women</u>.

One way to express compared persons or things is by using the conjunction **quam.** Note that this **quam** is not the relative pronoun. It has no antecedent and does not replace a noun. It connects two compared terms. The word that follows **quam** must be identical in case to the other (previously mentioned) person or object in the comparison.

As you translate the italicized words in the following sentences, pay close attention to the cases of the persons and things being compared.

1. We have never traveled *in a country more pleasing than Italy.*

_____

2. I have never yielded *to an enemy fiercer than you,* Minos.

_____

3. They had fought *with soldiers braver than these.*

_____

4. Brutus was *a nobler Roman than the other Romans* who killed Caesar.

_____

    [Why did Shakespeare call Brutus the noblest Roman of them all?]

5. Plutarch has written *that the life of the Spartans* was harder than the life of the Athenians**.*

_____

    * Spartānōrum
    ** genitive plural *Athēniēnsium*

LESSON LXII

BAUCIS ET PHILĒMŌN

 Formation of adverbs Adverbs, like adjectives, are able to express degree. However, they are not inflected forms because they do not have to agree with the words that they modify. Not all adverbs can be compared. Consider **semper** and **fortasse.**
To form the positive degree of an adverb drawn from an adjective, recall the declension to which the adjective belongs. If it belongs to the first or second declension, add **-ē** to the base. If it is a third declension adjective, then add **-iter** to the base.

Following the pattern illustrated in your textbook, give the Latin form of each adverb.

1. publicly _____

2. gratefully _____

3. nobly _____

4. commonly _____

5. equally _____

 Formation of adverbs Practice forming more adverbs from the following adjectives. Although you have not encountered these words yet, they are easy to master and helpful to know. Be prepared to translate the positive adverbs that you create.

		POSITIVE ADVERBS	TRANSLATION
1. dēnsus	(thick)	_____	_____
2. tepidus	(warm)	_____	_____
3. frīgidus	(cold)	_____	_____
4. dulcius, dulce	(sweet)	_____	_____
5. crūdēlis, crūdēle	(cruel)	_____	_____
6. mollis, molle	(soft)	_____	_____
7. fēlix [gen., fēlīcis]	(happy, lucky)	_____	_____
8. acerbus	(bitter)	_____	_____
9. tenuis	(tenuous)	_____	_____
10. pauper [gen., pauperis]	(poor)	_____	_____

Comparison of adverbs To form the *comparative* degree of most adverbs, add **-ius** to the *base* of the positive form of the feminine adjective. (This is the same form as the comparative adjective, neuter nominative). To form the superlative degree of adverbs, add **-ē** to the base of the *superlative adjective*.

Translate each sentence with special attention to adverbs.

1. Līberius dīxērunt.

_____

2. Fortissimē pugnāverant.

_____

3. Prōcēdēsne celeriter?

_____

4. Victōria pūblicē nūntiāta est.

_____

5. Causam aptissimē agit.

_____

Remember that the ablative of manner is similar in meaning to adverbs. Translate each in two ways where possible.

6. With swiftness: **cum celeritāte**   *or*   swiftly

_____

7. with diligence   *or*   diligently

_____

8. with great enthusiasm   *or*   very enthusiastically

_____

9. with courage   *or*   courageously

_____

10. with much gratitude   *or*   most gratefully

_____

LESSON LXIII

DAEDALUS ET ĪCARUS

A **Comparison of adjectives: adjectives in -er** Some -er adjectives that you have learned include **integer, miser, pulcher,** and **sacer.** Most of these words are like **ācer** in the formation of their comparative forms, *i.e.,* they do not retain the letter **e** in their genitive singular base.

Which of these four words, on the other hand, is like **līber?**

_____

Identify the degree, case(s), and gender(s) of each adjective.

	DEGREE	CASE(S)	GENDER(S)
1. sacriōrī			
2. līberius			
3. integerrimae			
4. celere			
5. pulcherrima			
6. sacrārum			
7. līberrimī			
8. acriōrum			
9. miseriōre			
10. celeriōris			

B **Comparison of adjectives** Identify the degree of each phrase, and create its Latin equivalent.

	DEGREE	LATIN
1. too sharply		
2. very swift		
3. rather unhappily		
4. holiest		
5. extremely handsome		

C **Six adjectives ending in *-lis, -le*: irregular superlative** The *superlative* form of an adjective in its dictionary form, *i.e.,* masculine nominative singular, regularly ends in the letters __ __ __ __. These letters are preceded by double consonants such as __ __ in the case of the superlatives for **altus** and **fortis** or __ __ in the superlatives for **līber** and **ācer.**

A third pair of consonants *(ll)* precedes the superlative ending of six adjectives whose base ends in *l*: **facilis, facile** *(easy);* **difficilis, difficile** *(hard);* **similis, simile** *(like);* **dissimilis, dissimile** *(unlike);* **humilis, humile** *(low, humble);* and **gracilis, gracile** *(slander).* Actually, one of these *l'*s belongs to the base. It is worthwhile to memorize these six adjectives as a distinct subset of Latin superlatives.

Create the superlatives for the following regular third declension adjectives.

1. puerīlis *(childish)* _____

2. servīlis *(servile)* _____

3. facile *(easy)* _____

Examine the following list closely. Some of the entries are adjective bases for the *superlative degree* and some are not. Circle the letter that must be added between columns A and C in order to create the superlative form of each word. If this cannot be done with the word form in column A, circle "wrong base."

A	B				C
4. ūtilis . . .	l	r	s	wrong base	. . . imus
5. acr . . .	l	r	s	wrong base	. . . imus
6. similis . . .	l	r	s	wrong base	. . . imus
7. miser . . .	l	r	s	wrong base	. . . imus
8. humil . . .	l	r	s	wrong base	. . . imus
9. fort . . .	l	r	s	wrong base	. . . imus
10. celer . . .	l	r	s	wrong base	. . . imus
11. amīcus . . .	l	r	s	wrong base	. . . imus
12. nōbilis . . .	l	r	s	wrong base	. . . imus
13. familiār . . .	l	r	s	wrong base	. . . imus

D **Dative with adjective construction** Until this time, you have encountered the dative case endings primarily as a means of expressing indirect objects. However, they are also used in connection with adjectives like **amīcus** and **inimīcus** *(friendly or unfriendly to).*

For each English word, supply a dative form. Then translate each with the given adjective.

1. amīcus (to the foreigners) **DATIVE** _____

_____

2. aliēnus (to the king) **DATIVE** _____

_____

3. dissimilis   (to many)   **DATIVE** _____

_____

4. finitimus   (to the mountains)   **DATIVE** _____

_____

5. grātus   (to all)   **DATIVE** _____

_____

6. inimīcus   (to a sister)   **DATIVE** _____

_____

7. secundus   (to no one)   **DATIVE** _____

_____

8. sacer   (to the goddess)   **DATIVE** _____

_____

9. similis   (to this)   **DATIVE** _____

_____

10. ūtilis   (to the nation)   **DATIVE** _____

_____

LESSON LXIV

DĒ PYRRHŌ ET EIUS VICTŌRIĀ

 Vocabulary Bene, which you saw for the first time in Unit I, does not end in a long **-e.** Neither does the positive adverb of **malus (male).**

Translate.

1. Pilam* bene iacit, sed male capit.

_____

   *pila, -ae, f. *ball*

 Derivatives: irregular comparatives and superlatives You have no doubt noticed that the irregularly compared Latin adjectives are the source of many familiar English derivatives. Drills with these derivatives are a good way to help you remember these new forms.

Circle the word that correctly completes each sentence.

1. If you come to school expecting the *worst,* you are a _____.

   a. extremist   **b.** minimalist   **c.** pessimist   **d.** pluralist

2. The winners of a class election are supported by a *larger* portion, or _____, of voting classmates.

   a. majority   **b.** minimum   **c.** priority   **d.** ultimatum

3. If you compare yourself unfavorably to others, as if you were *lower* in some way, you have an _____ complex.

   a. amelioration   **b.** approximation   **c.** inferiority   **d.** minority

4. To be named class valedictorian is to reach the *highest* point, or _____, of one's academic career in high school.

   a. benefit   **b.** pejoration   **c.** primacy   **d.** summit

5. A well-rounded education is a defense against _____, the tendency to diverge *very far from* the truth.

   a. extremism   **b.** minimalism   **c.** optimism   **d.** superiority

Choose a verb from the list that expresses the meaning of the italicized words in each sentence.

ameliorate	externalize	maximize	minor
approximate	major	minimize	optimize
benefit	malign		

6. Government and private enterprise strive together to *make* living conditions better for our country's poorest citizens.

_____

7. In their forecast, national interest polls try to *come close* to the opinions of the nation at large.

_____

8. City commissioners shape policies that will *serve* their communities *well.*

_____

9. Many political candidates gain popular support by promising to make taxes as *small* as possible.

_____

10. Aspiring politicians should take a *larger* number of their college courses in political science.

_____

Choose an adjective from the list that expresses the meaning of the italicized words.

approximate	inferior	optimal	pessimistic
exterior	maximum	pejorative	ultimate
extreme	minor		

11. Athletes are always happy to compete on the *best possible* playing surface.

_____

12. Certain sports commentators seem to dwell on the declining or *worsening* aspects of players' performances rather than on their better moments.

_____

13. There are many athletic infractions that carry *very large* penalties.

_____

14. Famous baseball teams in the American and National Leagues often maintain *smaller* clubs in other cities.

_____

15. To win a gold medal in the Olympics is to attain the *farthest* limit of an athletic career.

_____

Irregular superlatives Circle the correct response to each question.

1. Quid est pessimum?

   a. a hangnail   **b.** a broken finger   **c.** a severely frostbitten hand

2. Quid est maximum?

   a. a trilogy   **b.** a novella   **c.** a short story

3. Quid est minimum?

   a. nickel   **b.** penny   **c.** dime

4. Quid est plūrimum?

   a. 5/8   **b.** 3/4   **c.** 15/16

5. Quid est optimum?

   a. an A on a quiz   **b.** a C on a unit test   **c.** an F on a final exam

 Translate each prepositional phrase without using the genitive case.

1. on top of the mountain

   _____

2. at the end of the road

   _____

3. with the rest of the citizens

   _____

4. in the middle of the camp

   _____

5. next to the sea

   _____

LESSON LXV

PYRRHUS ET FABRICIUS

 Reflexive pronouns Remember that personal pronouns (first and second persons) can also be used reflexively.

Translate.

1. Mē expedīvī.

_____

2. Vidēsne tē clāre?

_____

3. Inter nōs dē hīs ēgimus.

_____

4. Vōs dēfendite.

_____

5. Is mē accūsat, sed ego mē nōn accūsō.

_____

 Reflexive pronoun of the third person The reflexive pronoun for the *third* person cannot be a form of **is, ea, id** *(he, she, it)*. The special reflexive words **suī, sibi, sē, sē** *(gen., dat., acc., abl.)* are used instead to mean *himself, herself, itself,* and *themselves.* The meaning *depends on what the subject of the verb is.*

Ea eam fefellit.	*She deceives her.*
Ea sē fefellit.	*She deceives herself.*

Note that a reflexive pronoun, by definition, *reflects* action back to the subject of a sentence. Since the reflexive pronoun serves as a target of action, it naturally completes the meaning of the verb in a sentence.

The intensive **ipse,** which is used only for emphasis, *may be omitted from a sentence without rendering it incomplete.* Compare the following.

Tē laudās.	*You praise yourself.*
... laudās	*You praise . . . (incomplete)*
Ipsa tibi crēdō.	*I myself believe you.*
Tibi crēdō.	*I believe you. (complete)*

Do not confuse forms of **suī** meaning *himself, herself, itself,* and *themselves* with forms of **suus, -a, -um** *(his (own), her (own), its (own) their (own)).*

Choose the correct responses.

1. Which of the following is not a form of the reflexive pronoun?

    a. sibi   **b.** suī   **c.** suās   **d.** sēsē

2. Which of the forms below would be used to translate the following sentence?

She wrote the letter herself.

    a. sua   **b.** suās   c. ipsa   **d.** sibi

3. Indicate which of the forms below could not be used in a translation of the following sentence.

I myself have betrayed myself.

    a. ego   **b.** ipse   c. mē   **d.** mihi

4. Which sentence(s) *must* use **vōs?**

    a. Have you students prepared for this competition?

    b. Have you prepared yourselves for this competition?

    c. Have you yourselves prepared for this competition?

5. Which one of the four forms listed below would all three of the following sentences use?

The Amazon women were urged on by their queen.
The Britons were urged on by their queen.
The men and women of Carthage were urged on by their queen.

    a. suā   **b.** suīs   c. sē   **d.** suārum

 Reflexive pronoun of the third person Translate each sentence, observing the case of the reflexive pronoun in each. The subjects of the sentences name Rome's first imperial dynasty.

1. Post mortem Iūlī Caesaris Octāvius sē C. Iūlium Caesarem Octāviānum appellāvit.

_____

_____

2. Tiberius uxōrem suam Iūliam sēcum Capreīs* nōn habitāre cupīvit.

_____

on Capri (an island)

3. Caligula partem suī dīvīnam esse crēdidit.

_____

4. Claudius statuit sē in Britanniā bellum gessūrum esse.

_____

5. Nerō regiam magnam sibi cōnstruī* iussit et posteā hanc rēgiam Domum Auream appellāvit.

_____

_____

*from **cōnstruere** _to build_

D **Reflexive possessives of the third person** Supply a form of the reflexive possessive **suus** that translates the italicized word in each sentence.

1. Publius Cornelius Scipio received _his_ fourth name, Africanus, for his outstanding service in the Punic Wars.

_____

2. Lucius Aemilius Paulus received his fourth name, Macedonicus, for _his_ outstanding deeds in the Macedonian Wars.

_____

3. The Gracchi rivalled the reputation of _their (own)_ grandfather Scipio.

_____

4. Augustus said he would dedicate _his_ temple to Apollo.

_____

LESSON LXVI

RĒGULUS

 Declension of numerals When you first learned to count in Latin, you realized that most numerals in this language are indeclinable. In an earlier lesson, you learned the special forms of **ūnus.** This lesson essentially completes your introduction to Latin numbers.

Which endings of **duo** are not like the plural endings of **multus?**

_____

_____

On the other hand, note that the endings of **trēs** are exactly like the plural endings of **omnēs.** Give the Latin for the following.

1. one citizen's _____

2. for two neighbors _____

3. in three wars _____

4. one hundred ships   *(accusative)*   _____

5. one thousand roads   *(nominative)*   _____

6. two temples   *(accusative)*   _____

7. two thousand years   *(nominative)*   _____

8. one farmer   *(dative)*   _____

9. three envoys   *(nominative)*   _____

10. three thousand men   *(accusative)*   _____

 Numerals Answer each question in Latin. Some answers might come from classroom lectures or independent study projects, or you may need to consult a reference work. Page 502 in your textbook gives a full list of numerals.

1. How many heads did Cerberus have?

_____

2. How many muses were there?

_____

3. How many Roman consuls served at one time?

_____

4. How many months are there in a year?

_____

5. The Fates were deities who controlled the destinies of human beings. How many Fates were there?

_____

6. For how many years did the Greeks fight at Troy?

_____

7. In a professional football game, how many men are playing on both sides at any given time?

_____

8. How many fingers and toes do you have?

_____

9. How many states are there in the continental United States?

_____

10. How many eyes did Juno's beloved Argus have?

_____

11. After completing how many grades of high school will you finally be called a senior?

_____

12. How many times does the word *one* appear on the American one-dollar bill?

_____

13. How many years comprise a millennium?

_____

14. If you had ten bills in your wallet, all of which depicted Andrew Jackson, how many dollars would you have?

_____

C **Review of verbs** Complete the following synopses.

1. explicāmus	explicābāmus	_____
explicāvimus	_____	explicāverimus
2. _____	tribuēbam	tribuam
tribuī	tribueram	_____
3. trāduntur	_____	trādentur
_____	trāditī erant	trāditī erunt
4. perficitur	perficiēbātur	_____
perfectus est	_____	perfectus erit
5. _____	vincēbās	vincēs
vīcistī	vīcerās	_____

D **Translation** On pages 448–449 of your text, find the Latin equivalents of the following phrases. Be careful not to quote too much or too little.

1. if peace were not made

_____

2. he himself remained

_____

3. by whom he was killed

_____

4. he surrendered himself

_____

5. with a hundred elephants

_____

6. fighting against three generals

_____

7. many thousands of prisoners to be given back

_____

8. the enemies had no hope

_____

9. the senate, deeply moved by this advice

_____

10. to buy prisoners with gold

_____

CLASSICAL MYTHS AND PORTRAITS OF ROMAN HEROES

UNIT XII REVIEW

REVIEW

The following ten men were extremely important to the development of the Roman Empire. Match each to his capsule biography. Consult an encyclopedia if necessary.

Cato	Marius	Scipio Africanus
Gaius Gracchus	Mithridates	Scipio Nasica
Tiberius Gracchus	Petilius	Sulla
Hannibal		

1. Like Cicero, he was a **novus homo** and came from Arpinum. He fought at Numantia. He defeated the Cimbri. He married Julius Caesar's aunt.

   _____

2. He said "Beasts and birds have their holes and hiding places; the men who fight and die for Italy should also." He advocated land reform. In 132 B.C., he was murdered by his enemies in the senate.

   _____

3. He was considered the greatest of Roman orators before Cicero. He was elected tribune in 124 B.C., and continued the reforms begun by his brother.

   _____

4. He was a fearless soldier for twenty-four years. He was among the first great authors of Latin prose and is particularly remembered for his *de Agricultura*. He ended all his speeches in the senate with the words, **"Ceterum censeo delendam esse Carthaginem."** Ironically, he detested the man who accomplished his desire.

   _____

5. This man was a famous king of Pontus, an area in Asia on the southeast side of the Black Sea. He fought many times against the Romans. Two famous Roman generals contended over the right to bring war against him.

   _____

6. According to Livy, this man was "the first to enter the battle and the last to abandon the field." The truth of this statement was proven to the unfortunate Romans at Cannae and Lake Trasimene.

   _____

7. As a result of his victory at Zama, this general received a cognomen identifying the province in which the battle occurred.

   _____

8. This man led senators into the Forum to attack and kill his distant kinsman, the tribune for 132 B.C.

_____

9. At the instigation of a stern censor, this jurist required a prominent Roman figure to account for his use of loot taken in a war with Antiochus.

_____

10. As a Roman commander, he defeated a famous Asian king. He restored to the senate many rights that had been given to the plebs. He was called Fēlix *(fortunate),* in spite of the fact that he ordered the deaths of many Romans.

_____

ROMAN LEGENDS: PORTRAITS OF PERSEVERANCE, PATRIOTISM, AND COURAGE

MARIUS ET SULLA

 A **Accusative of extent of space/duration of time** You have already learned three uses of the accusative case: direct objects of verbs, objects of certain prepositions, and the subjects of infinitives in indirect statement. In this lesson, you are introduced to other uses of this case, including the accusatives of *extent of time* and *extent of space*. These are easily recognized constructions, since they deal with duration of time and distance.

A few units of measure will help you practice these constructions.

ulna, -ae, f.	*an ell*	*(a yard)*
uncia, -ae, f.	a *twelfth part of a whole*	*(an inch)*
mīlle passuum	*one thousand paces*	*(a mile)*

Translate each sentence.

1. Impluvium in illō atriō erat novem pedēs lātum.

_____

2. Multōs diēs ad montēs iter fēcimus.

_____

3. Vulnus quattuor unciās altum est.

_____

4. In forō verba paucās hōrās fēcit.

_____

5. Sex pedēs longum est et ā mīlite portātum est.

_____

6. Quattuor mensēs Prōserpina cum Plūtōne habitat.

_____

7. Hic ager centum ulnās longus est. Quid hīc* accidit?

_____

*hic *here*

8. Quī consul, annō 104 B.C., Iugurtham vīcit?

_____

9. Antīquīs temporibus, togās nōn gerēbant.

_____

B **Vocabulary: words frequently confused** Choose the word that correctly completes each sentence.

1. Ad urbem _____.

   a. accēdo   **b.** accidō

2. Ille est m_ior _____.

   a. aetāte   **b.** aestāte

3. _____ adest; aliī absunt.

   a. alius   **b.** alter

4. "_____ Rōmānus sum," Sānctus Paulus inquit.

   a. cīvis   **b.** cīvitās

5. Inter _____ animalium Āfricānōrum sunt crocodīlī et elephantī.

   a. gēns   **b.** genera

6. _____ fuistis?

   a. ibi   **b.** ubi

7. _____ causās bellī explicat.

   a. liber   **b.** līber

8. Spatium duōrum pedum nōn _____ ulnae (yard) est.

   a. pars   **b.** pār

9. Castra pōnere nōn _____.

   a. posuit   **b.** potuit

10. Hī _____ familiārēs erant.

    a. vīrēs   **b.** virī

LESSON LXVIII

GRACCHĪ

 Vocabulary: review of derivatives Be sure to return from time to time to Latin word lists from earlier units. It is almost impossible to learn all the good English derivatives from any one word when that word is still new to you. However, as you become more familiar with a Latin root, you will find it much easier to recognize its altered spelling and its basic meaning in everyday English words.

Complete each sentence with a word from the list.

appetite	impetus	perpetuate	petulant
compete	incompetent	petition	repeat
impetuous	perpetual		

1. It is difficult for a small school to _____, or contend equally, with a larger one.

2. Fame is a powerful _____, leading individuals to exert themselves in their quest for excellence.

3. The spoiled little boy often seemed _____ in his choices of activity, running to seek one new amusement after another.

4. In music, a symbol that resembles a colon tells an artist to go back to an earlier point in her score and to _____ a passage, or to play it once more.

5. The waves of the ocean seek the shore through age after age in a

_____ movement.

 Fourth declension nouns Answer based on your reading.

1. The nouns that are grouped together as a declension share certain case endings. Which case ending is the basis for assigning a noun to a particular declension?

_____

2. What is the ending for nouns of the first declension?

_____

3. What is the ending for nouns of the second declension?

_____

4. What is the ending for nouns of the third declension?

_____

The same rule applies to the fourth declension. You cannot recognize nouns of this group by their nominative singular forms. In fact, these forms may look like nouns of the second or even the third declension because the nominative ending is also **–us.**

EXEMPLĪ GRĀTIĀ

terminus   **corpus**   **manus**

However, a full vocabulary entry will show you two things about the words listed above: their respective declensions and their genders. Give this information for each of the preceding words.

GENITIVE _____   _____   _____

GENDER _____   _____   _____

It is always a good idea to compare new case endings to those you have already learned.

5. Two of the ten endings for the fourth declension are identical to endings of the third declension. What are they?

_____

6. What vowel is found in each of the remaining eight case endings?

_____

7. Which of the case endings is used three times?

_____

8. Which case ending differs only slightly from the one that is mentioned above?

_____

Case identifications Identify the declension, case, and number of each noun.

	DECLENSION	CASE	NUMBER
1. domum	_____	_____	_____
2. rēgum	_____	_____	_____
3. equum	_____	_____	_____
4. cāsuum	_____	_____	_____
5. senātuī	_____	_____	_____
6. studī	_____	_____	_____
7. tempus	_____	_____	_____
8. manus	_____	_____	_____
9. virtūs	_____	_____	_____
10. exercitū	_____	_____	_____

Name _____ Date _____

D **Agreement of fourth declension nouns** Give a form of **exercitus** that agrees with each modifier.

1. barbarī   _____

2. ēgregium   _____

3. premente   _____

4. illōrum   _____

5. totīus   _____

E **Syntax and case usage** After translating the passage on pages 468 and 469, complete the following. Match each word or phrase to its type of ablative.

1. _____ Dīligentiā   line 1   **a.** ablative absolute

2. _____ Domō petītā   line 3   **b.** accompaniment

3. _____ ā nōbilibus   line 8   **c.** agent

4. _____ mēcum   line 12   **d.** manner

5. _____ in somnō   line 14   **e.** place where

Match each noun with its case and use.

6. _____ Cornēliae   line 3   **a.** genitive possessor

7. _____ hospitae   line 5   **b.** indirect object

8. _____ ōrnāmenta   line 6   **c.** dative with special adjective

9. _____ plēbī   line 7   **d.** nominative subject

10. _____ aliī   line 12   **e.** predicate nominative

What is the case use for each of the following?

11. _____ eōs   line 9   **a.** accusative object of an infinitive

12. _____ sē   line 16   **b.** accusative direct object

13. _____ mīlitēs   line 18   **c.** accusative subject of infinitive

14. _____ cōnsilia   line 21   **d.** accusative of duration

15. _____ multōs annōs   line 22   **e.** nominative subject

Identify each verb form.

16. _____ dēspicientēs   line 11   **a.** present active participle

17. _____ venīte   line 12   **b.** imperative verb

18. _____ vīdisse   line 14   **c.** perfect passive participle

19. _____ perfectūrum esse   line 16   **d.** future active infinitive

20. _____ dēsertus   line 19   **e.** perfect active infinitive

LESSON LXIX

SCĪPIŌ

 Vocabulary: verbs with dative complements A number of verbs, such as **noceō** *(do harm to; harm)* also require nouns in the *dative case* to complete their meanings, rather than the more usual accusative case. However, it is often possible to rephrase the English sentence so that this usage can be understood.

EXEMPLĪ GRĀTIĀ

    Dominus nōn servō nocuit.   *The master did not harm the slave*
                                         (The master did no harm to the slave.)

For some time now, you have been able to translate sentences of this sort i.e., verbs plus datives that are not indirect objects.

EXEMPLĪ GRĀTIĀ

    Gallī illīs cessērunt.   *The Gauls yielded to them.*
    Tibi crēdō.   *I believe you.*

As a compound of the verb *to be*, which is intransitive, **praesum** *(to be in charge of)* naturally and logically takes no accusative case complement. Though its meaning seems to call for a genitive, the dative case is the grammatically correct case for this verb's object, which literally means "be in front for."

Translate.

1. Omnibus praeest.

_____

Other compound verbs may take both a dative and an accusative noun, for example, **praeficiō** *(put someone in charge of something).*

EXEMPLĪ GRĀTIĀ

    Senātus Caesarem rēbus mīlitāribus praefēcit.

2. Translate.

_____

The reason that praeficiō can take an *accusative* object in addition to a *dative* object is due to the fact that the uncompounded verb form *(verb form minus prefix)* is **faciō,** a verb that is *transitive. Transitive* verbs may take a direct object while *intransitive* verbs (e.g., **sum**) cannot. So, it is logical that this verb can have an accusative direct object and a dative as well.

Name _____ Date _____

B **Fifth declension nouns** The last of the five Latin declensions is the smallest of them all. Which vowel appears in all ten of the case endings for this declension?

_____

At this point, you can make important observations about certain patterns that extend throughout the case endings of all five declensions, e.g., the accusative singular. Give the accusative singular of each noun and notice their similarity.

1. silva _____

2. socius _____

3. salūs _____

4. senātus _____

5. speciēs _____

The accusative plural forms of masculine and feminine nouns are also similar from declension to declension. Give that form for each noun.

6. memoria _____

7. magister _____

8. māter _____

9. manus _____

10. spēs _____

Continue to observe these patterns by giving the ablative singular and genitive plural forms of each noun and comparing those forms.

	ABLATIVE SINGULAR	GENITIVE PLURAL
11. cūra	_____	_____
12. annus	_____	_____
13. pāx	_____	_____
14. mare	_____	_____
15. impetus	_____	_____
16. spēs	_____	_____

17. In which declensions do the dative and ablative plural forms of all three genders share the case ending **-īs?**

_____

18. In which declensions do the dative and ablative plural forms of all three genders share the case ending **-ibus?**

_____

19. Which of these two patterns described above do the dative and ablative endings of the fifth declension most closely resemble?

_____

Name _____ Date _____

C **Case identification** Circle each plural noun in the list. Remember that some forms can be both singular and plural.

pēs	reī	diēs	causās
cāsus	vīs	iūs	deī
rēgis	spēs	casīs	mīles
fīnium	deae	domuum	lūcēs
aetās	impetūs	lūdī	generum

D Choose the correct response(s) to each question.

1. The noun **diēs** can be modified by which three of the following adjectives?

   a. omnēs   **b.** paucōs   **c.** multī   **d.** pulchriōris

2. The noun **speciēī** can agree with which two of the following adjectives?

   a. grātō   **b.** amīcae   **c.** familiārī   **d.** vestrī

3. The noun **rēbus** *cannot* be used in which of the following constructions?

   a. direct object   **b.** indirect object   **c.** subject   **d.** possessor

4. Which of the following is *not* genitive?

   a. huius diēī   **b.** nūllī speī   **c.** omnium rērum   **d.** decem speciērum

5. Which is *not* dative?

   a. merīdieī   **b.** exercituī   **c.** lībertātī   **d.** frūmentī

238
    LATIN FOR AMERICANS, LEVEL 1
UNIT XIII LESSON LXIX

WORKBOOK
Copyright © by The McGraw-Hill Companies, Inc.

Name _____ Date _____

LESSON LXX

CATŌ ET SCĪPIŌ

 A **Case usage: prepositions and their objects** It is important to know which case each preposition governs. Let's review the entire list of prepositions you have learned. Choose the appropriate form of each object and then translate the phrase.

	FORM		TRANSLATION
1. ā	familiam	familiā	_____
2. ad	oppidum	oppidō	_____
3. ante	nōs	nōbīs	_____
4. apud	amīcōs	amīcīs	_____
5. circum	montem	monte	_____
6. contrā	hostēs	hostibus	_____
7. cum	amīcitiam	amīcitiā	_____
8. dē	senātum	senātū	_____
9. ē	lūcem	lūce	_____
10. in	domum	domō	_____
11. inter	exercitūs	exercitibus	_____
12. ob	impedīmenta	impedīmentīs	_____
13. per	undās	undīs	_____
14. post	labōrem	labōre	_____
15. prae	haec	hīs	_____
16. prō	populum	populō	_____
17. sine	vim	vī	_____
18. sub	aquam	aquā	_____
19. super	numerum	numerō	_____
20. trāns	regiōnēs	regiōnibus	_____

B **Genitive and ablative of description** Indicate whether or not each phrase would be more likely to be expressed in the genitive or ablative case. Review the criteria for making a correct selection in your textbook before beginning.

GENITIVE/ABLATIVE

1. a road of one hundred miles _____

2. a statue of great beauty _____

3. a man of few words _____

4. a coat of many colors _____

5. a race of 26.8 miles _____

6. a look of contempt _____

7. a sky of deep blue _____

8. a collection of twenty hit singles _____

9. a sea of unusual tranquility _____

10. an expanse of desert _____

ROMAN LEGENDS: PORTRAITS OF PERSEVERANCE, PATRIOTISM, AND COURAGE

UNIT XIII REVIEW

A **Dative of indirect object** Choose the correct grammatical form. You may wish to review your text first.

1. Mūnus _____ committam.

   a. eī   **b.** ad eum

2. Quis Galliam _____ iūnxit?

   a. imperiō   **b.** ad imperium

3. Territus, _____ contendī.

   a. templō   **b.** ad templum

4. Exercitum _____ redūcet.

   a. castrīs   **b.** ad castra

5. Captīvī _____ redditī sunt.

   a. suīs   **b.** ad suōs

6. Mīlitēs _____ accēdunt.

   a. portīs   **b.** ad portās

7. _____ dīcere nōn poteram.

   a. rēgīnae   **b.** ad rēgīnam

8. Lēgātus _____ mittētur.

   a. senātuī   **b.** ad senātum

9. Grātiam _____ ostendistis.

   a. hīs   **b.** ad hōs

10. Submittitne lūdus tuus _____ alium annum linguae Latīnae?

    a. tibi   **b.** ad tē

Roman biographical portraits The following ten men were extremely important to the development of the Roman Empire. Match each to his capsule biography. Consult an encyclopedia if necessary.

Cato	Marius	Scipio Africanus
Gaius Gracchus	Mithridates	Scipio Nasica
Tiberius Gracchus	Petilius	Sulla
Hannibal		

1. Like Cicero, he was a novus **homō** and came from Arpinum. He fought at Numantia. He defeated the Cimbri. He married Julius Caesar's aunt.

   _____

2. He said "Beasts and birds have their holes and hiding places; the men who fight and die for Italy should also." He advocated land reform. In 132 B.C., he was murdered by his enemies in the senate.

   _____

3. He was considered the greatest of Roman orators before Cicero. He was elected tribune in 124 B.C., and continued the reforms begun by his brother.

   _____

4. He was a fearless soldier for twenty-four years. He was among the first great authors of Latin prose and is particularly remembered for his treatise *dē Agricultūrā*. He ended all his speeches in the senate with the words, **"Ceterum censeō dēlendam esse Carthāginem."** Ironically, he detested the man who accomplished his desire.

   _____

5. This man was a famous king of Pontus, an area in Asia on the southeast side of the Black Sea. He fought many times against the Romans. Two famous Roman generals contended over the right to bring war against him.

   _____

6. According to Livy, this man was "the first to enter the battle and the last to abandon the field." The truth of this statement was proven to the unfortunate Romans at Cannae and Lake Trasimene.

   _____

7. As a result of his victory at Zama, this general received a cognomen identifying the province in which the battle occured.

   _____

8. This man led senators into the Forum to attack and kill his distant kinsman, the tribune for 132 B.C.

_____

9. At the instigation of a stern censor, this jurist required a prominent Roman figure to account for his use of loot taken in a war with Antiochus.

_____

10. As a Roman commander, he defeated a famous Asian king. He restored to the senate many rights that had been given to the plebs. He was called Fēlix *(fortunate)* in spite of the fact that he ordered the deaths of many Romans.

_____